Last Edens

OF AFRICA

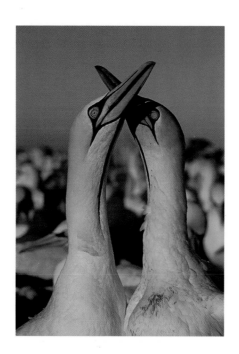

Last Edens
OF AFRICA

Liz Day • Francois Odendaal

PHOTOGRAPHS BY
Claudio Velásquez

SOUTHERN
BOOK PUBLISHERS

ACKNOWLEDGEMENTS

This book was only made possible with the support, encouragement, guidance and assistance (both logistic and financial)
of a large number of people and organisations, and our heartfelt thanks go to all of you. Companies and organisations to which we are particularly
indebted include (in alphabetical order): Abercrombie and Kent Safaris, Air Botswana, Air Madagascar, Air Malawi, Air Seychelles, Alexkor Ltd, ANGAP,
Central Wilderness Safaris, De Beers Consolidated Mines, Eco-Africa Environmental Consultants, Environment Department of the World Bank,
Fantasea, Global Environment Facility (GEF), Kalahari Kavango Safari Company, Kayak Africa, Madagascar Expedition Agency, Marine Science Program
of the Swedish Government, NAMDEB, National Geographic (Grant No. NGS 5539-95), Ruhija Research Centre, SAREC, SEACAM, SETAM,
Seychelles Island Foundation (SIF), SIDA/SAREC, South African Broadcasting Company (SABC), South African National Parks, Uganda Wildlife
Authority, Wild Frontiers, WWF Madagascar and the Zoology Department of the University of Cape Town, as well as to the governments
of Botswana, Namibia, South Africa, Uganda, Malawi, Seychelles, Madagascar, Mozambique and Tanzania, for allowing
us to catch a brief glimpse of those Edens of which they are the proud stewards.

Out of the many individuals who assisted us in various ways, often far beyond the calls of duty, friendship or even
sometimes dignity, the following stand out in particular, in alphabetical order: John Addison, Grant Anderson, Hutton Archer, Chris and Pam Badger,
Clive Bester and all those at his camp: Eben, Masie and Bushy, Phillipe Blaide, Lesley Boggs, George and Margo Branch, Marius Burger, Lindsay Chong
Seng, Jack Chilakalaka, Barbara Ciociola, Barry Clark, Joanne Daneel, John Day, Bruce Dell, Richard Dugmore, Roger Dugmore and his family, Neville
Eden, Papa Emile, Hannetjie Fourie, Paul and Jane Goldring, Paddy Gordon, Jill Gordon, Ida Hames-McNair, Kate Henderson, Christa Joubert, Donald
and Sally Kinross, Marcel Kroese, Maurice Lalanne, Wally Lange, Cathy le Grange, Olof Linden, Tim and Bryony Longden, David Lonsdale, Carl
Lundin, Paul Mann, John McNutt, David Moffat, Keith Musana, Tracey Phillips, Jean Pierre, Mike Picker, Louis Raubenheimer, Tiana Razafimahatratra,
Guy Rondeau, Naina Raharijaona and Bodo Ralantoarilolona, Callum Ross, Samson and the staff at the Bwindi Forest Camp, Nina Steffani, Floors
Strauss, Anthon van Eck, Emily and Francisca Velásquez, Dianne Waddle, Lydia Willems, Betunga Williams and the other guides at Bwindi Forest, Sarel
Yssel and staff at Mvuu, in Liwonde National Park. Special thanks to our filming and editing team: Riaan Laubscher, Tiny Laubscher, Steve Mannering
and Peet Joubert, as well as to the staff at Southern Books, and Louise Grantham, Reneé Ferreira and Alix Gracie in particular, for their patience, tolerance, assistance and creative input into all aspects of this book. A number of people agreed to review various chapters of this book, and their input,
insight and constructive criticisms are gratefully acknowledged: George Branch, Jenny Day, Penn Lloyd and Jeremy Midgely.

ISBN 1 86812 754 0

First edition, first impression 1998

Published by
Southern Book Publishers (Pty) Ltd
(a member of the New Holland Struik Publishing Group (Pty) Ltd)
PO Box 3103, Halfway House 1685

Cover design by Alix Gracie
Map by Alix Gracie
Designed and typeset by Alix Gracie
Set in Bembo 9/12pt
Reproduction by Hirt & Carter, Cape Town
Printed and bound by Kyodo Printing, Singapore

HALF TITLE PAGE: *A pair of Cape Gannets "fence" with their necks – a common display of mate recognition.*
TITLE PAGE: *The sun sets over the cold waters of the Benguela Current, off the Namaqualand coast.*
OPPOSITE: *A male lion drinks from a pan in the Kalahari Gemsbok National Park, South Africa.*
CONTENTS: *A male chameleon* (Furcifer pardalis) *from the Masoala Peninsula,
Madagascar, displays its brightly coloured markings.*

Contents

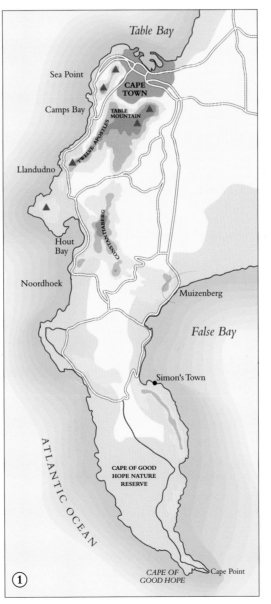

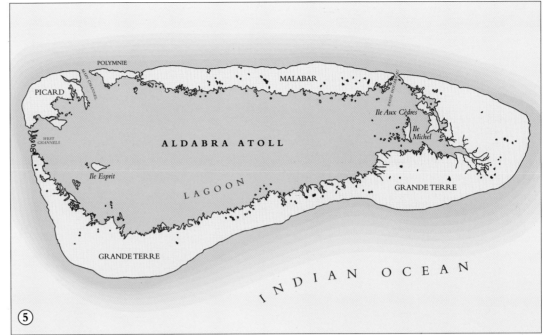

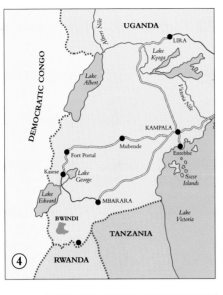

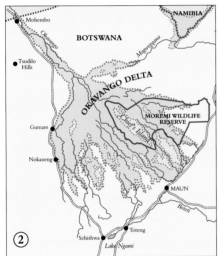

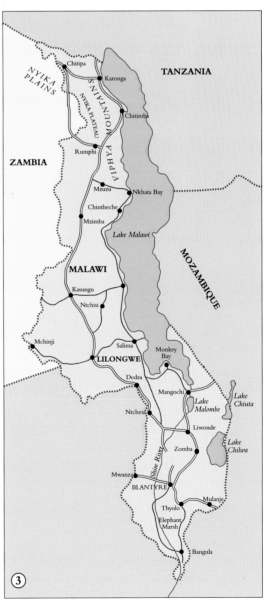

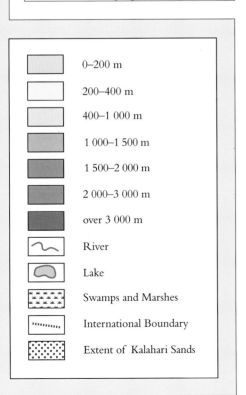

0–200 m

200–400 m

400–1 000 m

1 000–1 500 m

1 500–2 000 m

2 000–3 000 m

over 3 000 m

River

Lake

Swamps and Marshes

International Boundary

Extent of Kalahari Sands

Introduction

LEFT: *A thick undergrowth of luxuriant vegetation characterises this mist forest in Gongo Rouge.*
TOP LEFT: *Canopy of coco-de-mer – the Seychelles palm.*
TOP RIGHT: *Robber crab on the island of Aldabra, Seychelles.*
ABOVE: *Clouds pour over the top of Table Mountain, in the Cape Peninsula.*
RIGHT: *A moth displays fake "eyes" on its wings – a device to confuse its predators.*

Africa has long had the ability both to intrigue and astonish even the most seasoned traveller, and the ancient continent abounds in breathtaking landscapes, ranging from the largest and oldest deserts in the world to evergreen forests through which mighty rivers lazily wind their way to the sea. Near the equator, permanently snow-clad mountain peaks rise high above the clouds, standing eternal guard over the ancient valleys and plains, below which the human race had its earliest beginnings. Although many of these early humans remained in Africa to share the continent with the large mammals and their own primate ancestry, others fanned out to the furthest corners of the globe.

Prior to these events, which took place within the last hundred thousand years, Africa had already given rise to much more than the human race, being once the centre of a large landmass known as Gondwanaland. This supercontinent started to break up some 200 million years ago and pieces drifted away, giving rise to today's continents, as well as large islands such as Madagascar. Africa, however, still occupies the same position on the earth as it did when the break-up started. Straddling the equator, it contains a wide range of habitat types and today is home to an astonishing degree of cultural and biological diversity.

In the light of all this, it was with great enthusiasm and considerable trepidation that we accepted a dream assignment to make a documentary film series and produce this book on some of Africa's last wild places – an assignment that would involve journeys to distant and wonderful places that we had hitherto only dreamed of. As biologists, we knew that we were in for a great treat. Furthermore, exactly which destinations we would visit was to be our choice, the only prerequisites being that they should be relatively pristine and should contain spectacular biological diversity.

It was decided to focus upon places that collectively would reflect a degree of the diversity of landscapes found on the African continent and in the western Indian Ocean, referring to these strongholds of biological diversity as *The Last Edens of Africa*. The title was selected as a means of paying homage to the long evolved beauty of these places, while also hinting at their vulnerability to alteration at the hand of humans. To some extent, however, the whole of Africa can be considered an Eden, a place where the first humans lived in relative harmony with nature and were probably unable to inflict lasting damage on their environment through thoughtless or deliberate deeds.

The Edens described in this book cover only a handful of discreet localities, chosen by us as focal points for the book and film series. In that sense, many of them can be considered as islands surrounded by that large expanse of land that is Africa. To decide which specific places we would visit was indeed a difficult task, in part because there are so many of them, but also because the logistical problems of reaching many of them appeared almost insurmountable. For this reason we decided to start with the ones nearest to South Africa, where we live, so that our initial explorations of those sites not known to ourselves would be bolstered by the experience of colleagues who have worked there at some point during their research careers. Other sites were chosen because we came to know them intimately during the course of our own careers as biologists and were attracted to them in the first place because of their pristine nature and tremendous biological diversity.

The Cape Peninsula was included in the selection because it is home to the fynbos – part of the unique Cape Floral Kingdom that occurs only in the southern part of South Africa and has a floral diversity unequalled by any other botanical system in the world. The Kalahari thirstland, while famous for the San or Bushmen people who live there, was chosen because many parts of it remain largely unknown and few people venture into the heart of this unique dryland. In the remote north-west of South Africa lies another Eden – Namaqualand – in a region separated from the southern Namib Desert by the Orange River. Here, restricted to outsiders by the veil of security cast over it by diamond mining, exists a desert coastline second to none in its wildness and beauty.

Other places selected are similarly unique. In north-west Madagascar, a cloud forest linked by a river to a natural limestone fortress, defies the imagination of even the most wayward of ecologists. In the north east is found the last big rainforest in the country, its deep, dark interior untouched and devoid of any signs of human habitation. Other forests were also identified as Edens. In Uganda, the impenetrable forest of Bwindi, home to more than half of the world population of mountain gorillas, towers majestically above the surrounding sea of plantations.

Off the African continent we were lured by the island jewels of the Indian Ocean, particularly the granitic islands of the Seychelles and Aldabra, the largest coral atoll in the world. While from the African Rift Valley, the clear waters of Lake Malawi beckoned, with their rich variety of freshwater fish species.

From the hauntingly beautiful Cape Peninsula at the tip of Africa to the arid Kalahari, the Okavango Delta, Namaqualand, the forests, isolated islands, coral atolls and aquatic ecosystems, all of these Last Edens have one characteristic in common: they are blessed with astonishing biological diversity.

Reaching the Last Edens involved long journeys and rich experiences, affording ample opportunity to observe a continent that not only is the guardian and keeper of these special places, but whose own course will strongly influence the final destiny of the Last Edens themselves. While our focus was the Last Edens of Africa, we were fascinated by all aspects of the continent, in particular the ever-present striving by humans to eke out an existence in their environment, in a constant search for a means of living that would sustain them into the future. Time and again, the question arose as to whether this beautiful and unpredictable continent would learn to take charge of its own destiny before it was too late.

The task of filming our African odyssey was not always an easy one and our experiences were sometimes dangerous, sometimes amusing, but always exciting. Not surprisingly, the Last Edens were spectacular beyond our wildest imaginations. Visiting them awakened a spirit of adventure and discovery in each of us, and to film and write about them was not only a privilege but also a means of ordering our own thoughts and experiences. Yet there is no doubt that to experience the Edens fully one would need to go there oneself and stay for a longer time than we were ever able to. Consequently our attempts to convey their beauty and magnificence to a wider audience frequently invoked in us a feeling of powerlessness. The Last Edens and the long roads that often led to them left us with the strong realisation that we have seen but a tiny part of this magnificent continent on which we live, and awoke in us a powerful desire to see more of its last wild places. At the same time we know that no human being would be able to see them all, or even a fraction of them, constrained simply as we are by time and distance. Besides, Africa is a continent in a state of transformation. The Edens we have written about are fragile threads suspended between the past and the future. Africa's story still is being told. We deem ourselves fortunate to add a few words to that evolving story.

LEFT: *A full moon hovers over the Namaqualand shoreline.*
RIGHT: *Light shines through a cave entrance on Aldabra, Madagascar, highlighting ferns and mosses growing on the cave floor.*

CHAPTER 1

On the south-westerly tip of southern Africa, a fingerlike ridge of mountains juts out into the Atlantic Ocean. This is the Cape Peninsula, an unspoiled wilderness that rises above the clamour and smog of burgeoning Cape Town: an Eden seemingly more fragile for the constant reminder of the human threat baying at its heels.

View of Table Mountain from across Table Bay.

Waves crash on a Peninsula beach.

Bontebok at Cape Point.

THE *Cape Peninsula*

DIVERSITY FROM ADVERSITY

LEFT: *The rugged and exposed west coast of the Cape Peninsula, pounded by the waves of the Atlantic Ocean, extends south towards Cape Point.*
RIGHT: *A Cape sugarbird feeds on* Protea edima.

Known to early European sailors by a diverse array of names – the Cape of Good Hope, the Cape of Storms and The Fairest Cape – depending on conditions prevailing at their time of arrival, the Cape Peninsula and its abutting marine systems is a region of incredible diversity in terms of physical structure, climate and above all biological communities. Indeed, the tiny Peninsula is occupied by one of the most diverse groups of floral communities in the world – the Cape fynbos, 2 285 plant species of which occur in the Cape Peninsula itself.

Many of these species are endemic – that is, they occur in the south-western Cape and nowhere else in the world. Cape fynbos is, in fact, the vegetation most characteristic of the Cape Floral Kingdom – one of only six floral kingdoms in the world, and itself the richest floral kingdom, for its size in terms of species diversity, in the world.

The fynbos floral community is intricately linked in terms of both present function and evolutionary past to the physical structure and climate of its surroundings and its diversity is due in part to the peculiar characteristics of these parameters and to the variety of mechanisms developed by different species which enable them to exploit these conditions and in doing so, spread out to occupy a wide variety of different niches throughout the Peninsula. In particular, the land masses shaping the Peninsula have played a vital role in the development of biological communities within the region, by determining the strength and patterns of rain and wind and the availability of nutrient resources to the biota.

The making of a land mass

To trace the birth and growth of these impressive land formations it is necessary to go back some 1 000 million years, when the area that today includes the Cape Peninsula formed a shallow basin beneath the sea. Slowly, sediments began to accumulate in the basin and became, in time, the fine-grained shales of the Malmesbury Supergroup, still present in some of the oldest layers of the Peninsula today. A period of mountain building followed, during which these sedimentary layers were folded and elevated. In places, molten granite intruded through them, pushed up from the pressured bowels of the earth. Erosion followed, and the mountains were slowly whittled away to flat-topped plateaux.

Once again the earth underwent a cycle of sediment deposition, massive uplift and erosion, resulting at last in the flat-topped plateaux of the Cape Peninsula mountains as they are known today. The rocks typifying the more recent sedimentary layers are known as the Cape Supergroup and include the Table Mountain Sandstones. These ancient sandstones, forming layers as deep as 3 000 metres in places, play a pivotal role in explaining the patterns and ecosystem functioning of much of the Cape Peninsula today.

Formed from highly leached sands, the sandstones are low in nutrients, and so, therefore, are the soils deriving from them. The sandstones are also highly resistant to erosion and give rise to only a sparse cover of soil over the underlying rocks. These features are particularly important in explaining fynbos communities today, since organisms that inhabit this region require particular adaptations if they are to survive such frugal conditions.

Other factors also play a role in determining the ecological conditions under which the plants and animals must survive. The Cape Peninsula is subject to intense winds that sweep in from the south-east or, driven by frontal low pressure cells, move in from the north-west, preceded by banks of cloud and mist and often resulting in rain, particularly on the slopes of the coastal mountains. Overall the climate is Mediterranean, with cool rains falling during the winter months (June to September) followed by hot, dry summers when the south-easterlies rage across the mountains. Even during summer, however, the wind-driven clouds that sweep across the mountain tops and cascade down into the gorges bring with them moisture that condenses on stems and leaves, supplying a welcome supplement to the meagre rations of summer water.

The fynbos flora

Most of the plants on the mountain plateaux belong to the Cape Floral Kingdom, one of only six plant kingdoms found worldwide, and one with a phenomenally high species diversity. It comprises several groups of plant communities, one of which is known as fynbos. Although plants of the fynbos were used centuries ago for medicinal purposes by both San and Khoikhoi peoples, it derived its current name from the Dutch settlers in the Cape, who referred to it as *fynbosch*, meaning "fine bush". This name has been attributed both to the appearance of the fine, drought-adapted leaves of many of the plants of this biome, as well as to its inherent unsuitability as either a fuel or a timber wood – too *fyn* (slender) to be a timber resource.

While fynbos is not the only vegetation type that occurs within the Cape Peninsula, its ecological and conservation importance, as well as the intriguing array of adaptations it has evolved to cope with its particular environmental conditions, are all such that it deserves separate mention in any description of the natural systems of the Peninsula. Fynbos comprises three principal vegetation types, namely proteoid fynbos, heathlike or ericaceous fynbos, and restioid fynbos. Each growth form is rich in species and both their distributions and functioning are driven by three main forces: fire, summer drought and wind, and low nutrient availability.

Flowerland forged by fire

Fire was probably one of the most important factors leading to the development of fynbos vegetation in its present form. The increasing incidence of fire was directly related to changes in climate, such as the gradual drying out of the area, as well as in relatively recent years to increases in human populations in the region and an associated increase in burning. Prior to this, between two and five million years ago, a Mediterranean climate prevailed in the region and vegetation then was probably similar to, but not as diverse as, that of present times.

On the mountains, however, the thick forests belonging to former wetter eras still survived. A period of cyclical dry and wet seasons followed, known respectively as glacial and interglacial periods. The glacials lasted up to 100 000 years each and were interspersed with warmer, wetter interglacials, lasting only about 10 000 years. In general, the trend over the last 1,5 million years has been one of increasing dryness in southern Africa, causing the once lush Afromontane forests of the mountains to retreat slowly, stressed by drought and unfavourable conditions. As conditions gradually grew drier and vegetation became more prone to burning, fires – started primarily by lightning – became an increasingly frequent occurrence.

The rise in the incidence of burning had several significant effects. It reduced the range of the forests still further, to small relic patches surviving primarily in the protected gorges and ravines of the steep mountain slopes. It also led to the fragmentation of small pockets of plants, resulting in their diversification into area-specific species, and thus playing an important role in the proliferation of new fynbos species. Of particular importance, however, is the fact that the increased numbers of fires resulted in many fynbos plants evolving unique and intriguing adaptations towards coping with the new stress. At the same time, the decline of forests from all but a few areas freed up space into which the diversifying flora could expand. Not only did fire destroy existing forest species, but it also destroyed their seedlings, thus preventing their re-establishment. In later years, the arrival of timber-hungry settlers and sailors at the Cape led to the further reduction in forest trees.

OPPOSITE: *Sheer cliffs drop away and down to white beaches, sheltered coves and exposed, wave-torn reefs on the Cape Peninsula.*
FAR LEFT: *New growth quickly transforms a once fire-blackened landscape.*
LEFT: *Mosaics of ericas and restioses illustrate the rich diversity of the Peninsula flora.*
BELOW: *Near the coast, strandveld vegetation gives way to a new range of habitats – rocky shores, sand and sea.*

Plants growing in fire-prone regions are faced with very specific problems. They must either be able to withstand the searing heat and regrow after a fire has passed through the area, or they must possess some mechanism for protecting their seeds, so that a new generation will grow up after the fire. Plants that survive by producing seeds that are viable after fire are known as seeders, and include several proteoid species. Instead of releasing seeds into the environment immediately after fertilisation has occurred, many of these plants retain their seeds in tough, woody cones. The seeds mature slowly, only ripening in late summer when, due to the overall dryness of the vegetation, fires are most likely to break out. Fire serves as the stimulus for the seeds to be released from the cones. If no fires pass through the region for three or four years, the cones open of their own accord and release the old seeds onto the ground, where many are consumed by rodents.

Other seeders, such as species of *Mimetes*, have developed a different strategy for coping with burning. They drop their ripened seeds onto the ground and rely on small insects such as ants to carry them into their nests, where they will be protected from all but the hottest fires. This intriguing strategy is discussed in more detail later on in this chapter, but it is of interest to note that for some species, including *Mimetes*, fire is actually a prerequisite for germination. Only the heat from strong fires can penetrate the earth and crack the tough protective coatings of their seeds, thus freeing the seeds to grow up through the ground and into an environment from which most of the competitors for space have been temporarily removed.

Another group of fynbos plants, loosely termed the fire ephemerals, also produce seeds able to survive fires by being buried beneath the soil. After a fire they germinate quickly and themselves release large numbers of seeds. Such plants include the beautiful flowering lobelias, as well as the everlastings such as *Edmondia sesamoides*. The cue for germination of seeds of many of these species is smoke, and such plants rarely persist in the community for many years after a fire has passed through. Slowly, the plant community moves on to a new state, developing more and more woody vegetation which will, in time, fuel the next fire.

While seeders survive burning by protecting their offspring for the next generation, plants that are able to regrow after having been burnt, referred to as sprouters, employ a different tactic. The fynbos geophytes encompass one large group of sprouters. Geophytes are bulbous plants that are able to store water and nutrients within their tubers, protected beneath the ground. While the exposed

RIGHT: *The thick bark of this large* Leucospermum conocarpodendron *provides protection from burning.*
BELOW: *The symbolic red disa,* Disa uniflora, *adds a splash of colour to a mountain pool.*

ABOVE: *Open (right) and closed (left) cones of the* Leucodendron strolichinum. *The cones release viable seeds after fire.*
OPPOSITE LEFT: *The root parasite,* Hyobanche sanguinea, *also known as the cat's claw, obtains its nutrients from the roots of other plants.*
OPPOSITE RIGHT: Mimetes hirtus *in flower on the Cape Peninsula.*

leaves of the plant are destroyed by fire, the tuber itself usually remains unharmed. When the fire abates, leaving behind a blackened moonscape of charred twigs, the geophytes have a ready store of food and water at hand with which to promote the rapid growth of leaves and flowers. Moreover, with most of the vegetation burnt, competition at this time from other plants for nutrients, water and even pollinators is low.

The stored food of geophytes is useful even when fires do not raze the other vegetation to the ground. For one thing, it means that they still have the resources to flower when water is not readily available. Several species of geophytes thus flower in late summer and autumn, when very few other species are in flower and competition for pollinators is reduced. Members of the *Amaryllis* family (Amaryllidaceae) for example, use their resources to produce fleshy seeds in late autumn. The seeds need only survive until the wet winter, when the availability of moisture will assist their growth. Many species of *Gladiolus* also flower during autumn, a strategy that synchronises with the availability of their sole pollinator, the mountain pride butterfly (*Meneris tulbaghia*).

In the extraordinary fire-lily (*Cyrtanthus* spp.) the flexibility in geophyte flowering time is taken to extremes. These plants flower only after fire, independent of what time of year the fire occurs. Approximately two weeks after the vegetation has been reduced to a moonscape of grey-white ash and charcoaled twigs, the land erupts in a soft pink blaze of fire-lily blooms. The stimulus for flowering is believed to be provided by smoke.

Other members of the sprouter group include some of the larger fynbos shrubs, which resprout from subterranean buds after being burned or, during less intense fires, are protected by their thick layers of bark. Many of the restioids are also sprouters and burn right back, only to resprout a few short weeks later and grow back to their former dense stands.

Wind and summer drought

While fire played a role in establishing the fynbos vegetation, finalising the retreat of the forest trees into the sheltered mountain ravines and, today, in cycling the fynbos communities through periods of senescence, it is the climate of the region that forms the backdrop of daily or seasonal stresses with which the plants must cope. The Cape Peninsula has a true Mediterranean climate, with hot, dry summers that coincide with periods of maximum wind-intensity. This is of biological significance, because it means that water availability is at its highest during winter, when temperatures are too low for efficient plant growth to occur. For this reason, many fynbos plants flower in winter or spring when water is available, and grow during the drier but warmer summer. The strategy creates an evolutionary dilemma however, in that plants need to expose their leaf surfaces to the sun in order for photosynthesis (the production of food material from the sun's energy, carbon dioxide and water) to occur, while conservation of water resources requires that the total area exposed be minimised. Moreover, the desiccating effects of summer are exacerbated by the strong winds, which increase evaporative loss of water from plant surfaces.

Many plant species have evolved particular structures, such as waxy surfaces, hairs and scales, which serve to minimise water loss either by waterproofing the plant or by creating a sheen effect, to reflect more of the sun's heat off the plant. Amongst the ericoids, rolled leaves are another common adaptation towards reduced loss of water. Pores, or stomata, that allow gaseous exchange with the air, open into a chamber formed by the downwardly rolled leaf. Here, sheltered from the wind, water loss associated with gaseous exchange is kept to a minimum.

Not only do the strong winds of the Cape Peninsula increase desiccation through evaporative loss, but they also require plants to make structural adaptations to withstand their force. Thus most fynbos plants are either low-growing, or have long, flexible stems that bend easily.

While living in a wind-buffeted environment entails several costs to the fynbos plants, the power of the wind can also be utilised to advantage, and indeed wind plays an important role in effecting seed dispersal in many fynbos plants.

In the fynbos, where plant communities have few nutrients to spare for rewarding animal dispersers with fruit, harnessing the wind is a more viable option for dispersal. Wind dispersal does not require the production of fruit, and just about the only energetic input into the dispersal of such seeds is the development of small plumes or wings on the seeds, to increase their aerodynamic properties. These structures require few nutrient resources, comprising primarily carbon-based lignins and cellulose compounds. The ancient, leached and acid soils in fynbos areas have few nutrients to offer their floral communities, and plants that have survived in these conditions have done so largely by evolving a fierce frugality towards the utilisation of this precious resource.

Adapting to a low-nutrient environment

The paucity of nutrients within the fynbos soils has led to the development of ingenious methods for maximising what little there is. Many fynbos species have evolved mutually beneficial relationships with other organisms, such as fungi and bacteria, which are able to increase their uptake of nutrients (and nitrogen in particular) in exchange for shelter, support or carbohydrates. Bacteria on legumes, for example, stimulate the growth of tiny nodules on the plant's roots. Within these nodules, they make atmospheric nitrogen available to the plant in the form of organic nitrogen. In return, they receive carbohydrates from the plant, produced during the relatively "cheap" process of photosynthesis.

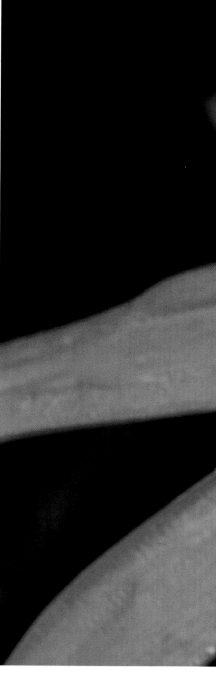

RIGHT: *A monkey beetle tunnels into a flower to feed on the nectar hidden within. As it feeds, hairs on its body trap pollen grains, which are then transferred to other flowers, and allow cross-pollination to occur.*

FAR LEFT: *Runway markings guide insects into* Agapanthus *flowers.*
LEFT: *Insects play an important role in the fynbos ecosystem. An ant crawls into a* Leucospermum *flower (above) while pollen-brushed hairs of the green protea beetle* (Trichostetha fascicularis) *transfer pollen from one plant to another (bottom).*

Similarly, in several proteoid species, bacteria and fungi bring about the growth of dense clusters of rootlets that are able to take up scarce or poorly soluble minerals from the soil, such as phosphorus, iron and manganese. Fungi and bacteria are not only involved in the uptake of precious nutrients and minerals, however. In some cases, they also protect the roots from pathogens and the effects of the low soil pH – another characteristic of fynbos soils.

As in any community, it is not surprising that many plant species have resorted to less savoury means of obtaining scarce resources. Several species of root parasites exist, for example, which obtain their nutrients from the roots of other more adept plants, such as the proteas. Other plants are carnivorous: the sundews (*Drosera* spp.), for example, have sticky, glandular hairs on their leaves, which are used to trap and digest insects, thus providing the plants with a rich protein supplement.

While accessing the maximum amount of nutrients available is of importance to plants, it is equally necessary that nutrient expenditure also be curtailed. The seasonal shedding of hard-earned leaf material, for example, has been largely eliminated by fynbos plants. Instead, the leaves grow slowly, and are dropped only occasionally, as they age. These old leaves collect beneath the plants, in dry, wind-rustled piles and the rapid nutrient cycle common to many other plant commun-

ities, whereby plant material dies and decays and the nutrients are reabsorbed by other plants, is a less common phenomenon in the fynbos ecosystem. Here, the long dry summers mean that decomposition occurs slowly, and the minerals and nutrients are released primarily when fires ravage the dry vegetation, releasing nitrogen in gaseous form, to be re-processed by bacteria within the soil.

Fynbos plants are also restricted by the shortage of nutrients in the pollination of their flowers, and the mechanisms they have developed rely on non-protein resources. In this process, wind is used by very few fynbos plants. For one thing, it requires the production of large amounts of pollen, only some of which is likely to land, by chance, on the receptive organs of another plant of the same species. In the fynbos, specialisation is the name of the game, with individual species occurring in very low numbers, restricted in some cases to one particular aspect of a mountain, or a particular kind of crevice. Under such circumstances, the expenditure of precious resources on the production of large amounts of pollen would be a needless waste, and the majority of fynbos plants rely instead on animals to effect pollination.

Competition for pollinators is fierce amongst these plants, and this competition is largely responsible for the astounding diversity of fynbos flowers. The colours, shapes and perfumes of the different blooms are meant to attract not the throngs of tourists that are drawn to the Cape Peninsula each year, but rather particular insects or animal pollinators. Nectar is the main ingredient used to draw these animals to the plant: a substance that is relatively cheap for the plant to produce, since it comprises primarily carbohydrates. Many plants are quite specific in the pollinator that they attract, and close associations have developed between different plants and their pollinators. For example, flower species that have long corollas (flower tubes) frequently attract insects such as horseflies with long proboscides that can be inserted down the long tubes. The sight of a horsefly desperately trying to angle its tediously long proboscis into a swaying flower in the full force of a south-easter is worth the necessary few hours of crawling on hands and knees through the fynbos.

Unusually, birds are also utilised in the pollination of some fynbos flowers. The Cape sugarbird (*Promerops cafer*) is one of the few bird species that is endemic to fynbos. Its long, sharp claws are highly effective in clinging to the waving flower stalks, even under severely windy conditions, and it has been suggested that the stout stems and flowers of several *Protea* species are adaptations towards supporting this relatively large bird as it feeds. The supply of energy-rich nectar is of great importance to these birds, for whom the act of flying expends a lot of energy. Sugarbirds may visit as many as 300 flowers a day, making them effective distributors of pollen between different flowers, and thereby ensuring cross-pollination.

Pollination is not only effected by the birds and insects of the sunlit hours. By night, the fynbos is transformed into a land of diverse odours – sweet, herbal, musky or even downright unpleasant. Yeasty odours coming from ostensibly drab flowers attract a suite of nocturnal rodents to the plant. The flowers usually open close to the ground and produce bowl-shaped supplies of sucrose by way of payment for pollination. For the rodents, the extra food source is often well-timed, coming when their usual diet of seeds is in short supply.

Butterfly pollinators are generally rare in the fynbos vegetation, with the exception of the endemic mountain pride butterfly (*Meneris tulbaghia*). This scarcity is mainly due to the predominance of tough leaves on many fynbos plants, which are unpalatable for the caterpillar stage of the butterfly life-cycle, as well as to the fact that winds are often stronger by day and impair the butterflies' ability to fly. Moths are thus a more common pollinator here. At night, it is argued, the winds often drop, and moths hone in on the pale-coloured flowers in the relative darkness.

The next generation

It is only in the production of seed material that the fynbos plants dispense with their frugality, and they invest heavily in laying up a store of lipids to aid in the survival of the young seedlings. Protea seeds, for example, are large and contain quantities of nutrients so that the seedlings will be able to grow quickly. Ironically, this store of protein also spells doom for a large proportion of the precious seeds: during the long dry summers, and particularly after fires, small rodents as well as many species of insects thrive on the rich bounty of seeds cast off by the plants.

Again, it is an integral feature of fynbos that diverse mechanisms should have been found by different species of plants to minimise, or even take advantage of, the vulnerability of the seeds. Many proteoids, for example, have developed a strategy known as serotiny, whereby they retain their seeds on the parent plant, stored within tough woody cones. Within the cones, the seeds are protected not

only from fire but also from the majority of predators. They are released en masse after fire, which is an advantageous time to open, as after the devastation of a fire, seed eaters (such as mice) are rare and the vegetation cover is sparse, giving the freshly dispersed seeds a brief window of advantage.

On the other hand, some species of proteas actually attract insects to feed on their seeds, by producing a fleshy, nutrient-rich attachment called an elaiosome. Species of ants, such as the pugnacious ants (*Anoplolepis* spp.) carry these protein reserves into their nests. There they feed on the choice elaiosomes, leaving the seeds themselves buried within their nest, where they are protected from fire. In the nest, the formic acid normally exuded by the ants acts as a fungicide and thus protects the seeds from decay.

Unfortunately, this strategy has backfired somewhat in recent years with the introduction of the alien Argentine ant (*Iridomyrmex humilis*). Not only does this species compete with indigenous ants, but it has a different feeding strategy, consuming the rich elaiosomes out in the open and leaving the stripped seeds vulnerable on the surface, to be eaten or destroyed by fire.

Animal browsers

It is not just the presence of the alien ant species that constitutes a threat to fynbos plants. The impact of herbivores in general is potentially fatal. With leaf material at a premium, plants can ill afford to lose leaves to browsing animals and many have thus developed a variety of mechanisms that serve to discourage grazers. At the same time, with food resources in the fynbos being scarce at best, herbivores have developed mechanisms to defeat the plant defences. The result is what is often referred to as an evolutionary arms race, with plants evolving mechanisms to deter herbivores, and herbivores adapting and overcoming the defences of the plant. Thus some species of herbivorous insects, for example, will still be found in large numbers on highly toxic plants.

Different forms of plant defences include the use of thorns, and tough leaves rich in lignin or cellulose as well as the so-called secondary compounds, made from readily available carbohydrates. These compounds include the waxy and indigestible waterproof layers of many plants. Over and above this, some plants have developed compounds with unpleasant odours or even toxic properties to deter herbivores. One of the most common groups of organic compounds produced by fynbos plants is tannin, a highly indigestible material that makes feeding on plant material an inefficient process for herbivores.

It is probably because of the scarcity of digestible food resources that there are generally so few animals in the fynbos although rodents are abundant, taking advantage of the one resource that is plentiful – the annual crop of fynbos seeds. The larger herbivores comprise primarily browsers, such as the small duiker (*Sylvicapra grimmia*) and the nocturnal grysbok (*Raphicerus melanotis*). Their long, slender muzzles are specially adapted to facilitate browsing among the small-leaved fynbos shrubs. In the south of the Cape Peninsula, the larger bontebok

(*Damaliscus dorcas dorcas*) occur. Once brought to the brink of extinction by hunting and large-scale habitat loss, these animals, whose numbers are now on the increase, are endemic to the south-western lowlands of the fynbos region.

Chacma baboons are another common feature of the south Peninsula and in fact have achieved a curious status of their own here, by becoming, in all probability, the only group of primates in the world other than humans to forage in the intertidal zone for seafood. When food is short, they converge on the sea shore for a seafood extravaganza, picking off limpets and mussels from the exposed rocks at low tide. Natural enemies of baboons are leopards, the largest predators of the fynbos region. Once common on the mountain slopes, few if any remain here today. More common smaller predators include large-spotted genets, as well as the rooikat or caracal.

The fresh waters of the Peninsula

As well as discouraging herbivores and thus influencing the whole herbivore/predator structure of the fynbos, tannins also form an important distinguishing feature of the freshwater systems of the Cape Peninsula. Tannins are water soluble, and as fynbos plants decay, the compounds leach out of their leaves and drain slowly through the soil until they enter the ground water. From here, they drain into the streams flowing off the sides of the Peninsula mountain ranges, imparting a dark, tea-coloured tint to the water and leading to the term "black waters" for such systems. In the Cape of Good Hope Nature Reserve, a number of freshwater pools exist in which the water is so dark that one's finger tips disappear from sight in the inky waters, before the wrist is even wet. As a result of the nature of the rocks through which they percolate, most Cape fynbos stream water is also acid, with some systems having a pH of less than 4.

On the flat tops of the Peninsula mountain ranges, sponges and seeps are a common feature of the landscape, where they result in thick stands of wetland vegetation comprising restioses, sedges, reeds and other plants, such as the tuberous arum lily (*Zantedeschia aethiopica*). The arum is found in most damp areas on the Peninsula and in the surrounding regions. In spring its beautiful white flow-

ers are home to the endangered arum lily frog (*Hyperolius horstocki*), which takes on a white colour and camouflages itself against the lilies, reverting to a drab brown during the dry summer and autumn and taking refuge amongst the withered wetland vegetation.

Many of the springs and seeps of the upper plateaux develop into small streams and drain down the steep mountain gorges. Here, covered by dense canopies of relic forest, the black waters trickle over large boulders and fallen trees, the steeply graded stream bed forming a range of habitats for the diverse array of aquatic organisms that are found within them. Sunlight is limited beneath the canopy, and ferns and mosses form the main component of the understorey.

Within the river, the larvae of numerous insects carry out their struggles for survival within their aquatic microcosms. Particularly notable amongst them are the amphipods (species of *Paramelita*), tiny shrimp-like creatures that inhabit mountain streams, feeding in large numbers on decaying leaves. Certain species of amphipods are endemic to single streams.

Many of the mountain streams of the Cape Peninsula are seasonal, flowing only for a few months during the winter and spring. Others flow slowly during summer, but in winter, after heavy rains have fallen in the upper catchment, these quiet trickling havens are transformed overnight into raging torrents that leave piles of debris high in the riverside trees, a startling reminder during the calm summer months of the dramatic seasonal changes in the system.

During winter, too, another phenomenon of the fynbos rivers manifests itself. As the flood waters rage over the river bed, frothy piles of dirty yellow foam are produced. As the water subsides, the foam is deposited on the rocks where, high in organic nitrogen and carbohydrates, it forms a source of food for many tiny aquatic organisms. This unexpected food resource is thought to result from the water table rising during the winter floods, flushing out the organic material contained in the ground water.

As the rivers flatten out in their lower reaches, their ecosystems change. Originally, many merged into wetlands where, the soils stabilised by stands of thick vegetation such as the well-adapted palmiet reed (*Prionium serratum*), the waters were able to spread out across a wide area and filter slowly down towards

OPPOSITE: *Blackwater streams run down through deep shaded gorges on the side of Table Mountain.*
RIGHT: *Amphipods occur in high densities in the mountain streams, where they feed on decaying leaves.*
BELOW: Rana fuscigula – *one of the most common frogs of the Peninsula.*

LEFT: *Pools of blackwater are a feature of the flat mountain plateaux.*
BELOW: *Water trickling over exposed rock faces on the mountain top result in patches of lush greenery.*

the sea. Such systems provided a natural buffer against the floods rampaging from the steep mountain catchments. Today, however, many of these wetlands have been lost to developments, although there are still some Peninsula rivers that retain vestiges of their former natural state. Indeed, a few are still able to provide habitats for semi-aquatic mammals such as the elusive Cape clawless otter (*Aonyx capensis*), the spoor and spats of which are more often seen than the animals themselves. These otters are as at home in the sea as in the rivers, and feed on both freshwater and marine produce, their dung piles of mussel and freshwater crab shells bearing testimony to their catholic choice of foraging areas.

Marine life of the Peninsula

The Cape Peninsula boasts a considerable variety of marine life-forms, from the tenacious limpets of the intertidal shores to the whales and dolphins that seasonally grace the seas, and the seals that breed in colonies on small, rocky islands off the mainland. Beds of kelp (primarily *Ecklonia maxima*, a tall, fronded seaweed) form aquatic forests that fan out from the rocky shores in a broad belt some 50 metres wide in places. These kelp beds provide habitat for inshore reef fish, such as red roman (*Chrysoblephus laticeps*) and the ubiquitous hottentot (*Pachymetopon blochii*), as well as the amazingly camouflaged klipvissies (mainly species of *Clinus*). These fish loll in clumps of similarly coloured seaweed, their frilled fins and fronded tails moving seaweed-like in the current.

MARINE GARDENERS OF THE PENINSULA

It is not only the plants and animals of the fynbos region of the Cape Peninsula that form close symbiotic relationships. On the low to shallow subtidal shores of the rocky intertidal, pear-shaped limpets (*Patella cochlear*) attain phenomenal densities – sometimes as high as 2 600 animals per square metre. These animals are grazers, and the question as to how they find sufficient grazing material on the rocks to support such high densities is an intriguing one. The answer lies in the patterns of encrusting algae that encircle each mature limpet. These algae are white, tough and barren looking, and form a flat layer over the rock surface. Whereas in other zones they form but one of many algal species with which they compete for space, in the cochlear zone they occur in monospecific stands, and each limpet is fringed with a raised ring of the algae. The limpets feed on this fringe, grazing it as it grows. Like lawn, the faster it is cut the faster it grows, and constant cutting reduces the number of other species present. Thus in a mutually beneficial arrangement, while the limpet is assured of a constant supply of "home-grown" food, the habitat is kept free of algal competitors.

ABOVE: *Sunlight touches the waves at Scarborough beach.*
LEFT: *Jackass penguins return to their breeding beaches after a foraging trip in False Bay.*

Within the kelp forests, numerous invertebrate animals enact their daily struggle to feed, breed and occupy a small patch of rock or seaweed frond. Some, such as the cryptic sponge crabs (members of the family Dromiidae), make efforts to camouflage themselves from the throngs of eager predators in this aquatic realm. They cultivate unpleasant-tasting sponges on their backs that deter predators out for a snack and serve to camouflage the animal at the same time.

While sponge crabs maintain a low profile, other animals such as the gaudily coloured nudibranchs, or sea slugs (of the genus *Opistobranch*), advertise that they are toxic or unpalatable. In many cases, the toxins are derived from feeding on small stinging marine organisms and absorbing their stinging cells. The cells lodge within the nudibranch, with unpleasant consequences for predators.

By contrast to these strategies, some kelp-bed invertebrates rely on the charity of others for protection. Abalone (*Haliotis midae*), for example, a valuable shellfish resource in the Western Cape, are brightly coloured as juveniles, their turquoise shells standing out clearly against the pale pinks and whites of the coralline-coated rocks. This conspicuousness, combined with their soft shells and delicate flesh, make them vulnerable to many predators, which they avoid by taking refuge under the prickly spine canopies of sea urchins (*Parechinus angulosus*). There they remain, feeding on kelp trapped by the urchins, until they are large enough to survive on their own. At this stage they crawl out and disappear into large cracks and crevices, only emerging into the open once they have grown a camouflaging layer of seaweed and sponges over their now toughened shells and are large enough to cling to a home scar from where they feed on kelp fronds trapped beneath their feet.

It is not only invertebrates that thrive in the oceans off the Cape Peninsula. Each year, pods of southern right whales (*Balaena glacialis*) and humpback whales (*Megaptera novaeangliae*) converge in the sheltered waters of False Bay to calve. Here they remain for a few weeks in late spring, only moving on to more exposed feeding grounds when the calves have achieved some competence in breaching, blowing and other activities of the whale realm.

Closer inshore, the fish life of False Bay encourages a thriving population of jackass penguins (*Spheniscus demersus*), which have established a breeding colony in a small, sheltered bay. Here, females produce up to two young each season. The siblings are born at different times, and if food becomes limited, only the older one will be fed and the younger bird sacrificed.

Life on the intertidal shores

The Cape Peninsula is blessed with a diverse shoreline that provides habitat to a range of intertidal organisms, and hence food to a whole sphere of bird, baboon and otter predators. Old kelp fronds and other organic material wash up on the sun-whitened, fine-grained sand of the beaches and fester in the sun. As they rot, they are set upon by thousands of beach scavengers: tiny amphipods, or beach hoppers (*Talorchestia capensis*), marine relations of the riverine amphipods, encrust the sheltered surfaces of the rotting material in their thousands and feed on it. Amphipods are laterally compressed versions of isopods, another animal that scurries in its millions at low tide among the intertidal rocks of the west coast, where they too scavenge for food beneath the shallow rocks.

The intertidal rocks are also home to several species of limpets, which occur in distinct zones down the shoreline towards the sea. On the high shore, the false limpets (*Siphonaria capensis*) clamp their moist muscular feet onto the dry rocks, to reduce desiccation beneath the fierce Cape sun. Here, exposed for several hours each day when the tide is out, they are vulnerable to predation, particularly by birds. In fact, however, suprisingly few fall prey to foragers, largely because of the unpalatibility of their flesh. When this is damaged, tiny pores within their mantles release a thick, white oozing fluid that probably acts as a deterrent to predators. On the low shore, the domed shells of granite limpets (*Patella granatina*) rise up in densely packed stands. Here they feed on both kelp debris and micro-algae growing on the rock faces. Lower still down the shore, the pear limpet (*Patella cochlear*) occurs in a distinct zone, each individual surrounded by a ring of encrusting coralline algae.

False Bay and the Cape of Storms

Technically speaking, it is the barren rocks of Cape Agulhas to the east of the Cape Peninsula, being the most southerly part of Africa, that mark the meeting place of the Atlantic and Indian Oceans. In fact though there is some justification for believing that the actual meeting point of the two oceans is in reality Cape Point. For much of the year, the warm Agulhas current, swinging down from the tropics of the east coast of Africa, extends as far as False Bay. Meanwhile the cold Benguela current flows up the coast of Africa, passing on the west of Cape Point. The distinction in marine systems between east and west coasts of the Peninsula is startling, with the head-numbing icy waters of the west coast providing a chilling contrast to the warmer waters of False Bay.

As surprising as the difference in marine systems is the difference in sea condition between the two sides. The mountain range that extends the length of the Peninsula means that the south-easterlies that ravage False Bay (so named a few centuries ago when a group of travel-weary sailors mistook it for Table Bay and the end of their journey) signal protection and balmy beaches on the west coast. On such days the long white beaches of the west dip into turquoise waters of astounding clarity, reminiscent – until the temperature takes one's breath away – of the tepid waters of a Grecian island. By contrast, when the rain-bearing north-westerlies whip the Atlantic Ocean on the west into a foaming torrent, with eight-metre waves that crash and foam against the hard black rocks, False Bay lies calm, its grey-green waters barely breaking as the swell ripples into the protected bays that mark its coast.

It is on the west coast that the exposure of the shoreline and the energy of the sea combine to provide conditions in which filter feeders can thrive. Filter feeders rely on a constant supply of organic particles in the water, which they filter out and digest. The rate of growth of the organism depends both on the concentration of organic particles in the water, and on the rate at which fresh solutions are turned over. On the west coast, both these factors are favourable and have led to thriving populations of mussels, the black-shelled Mediterranean mussel (*Mytilus galloprovincialis*) in particular. However, far from being a positive sign of the lush marine resources of the Cape Peninsula, this species is actually an invasive alien mussel, probably brought inadvertently to South Africa some 30 years ago from the Mediterranean, attached to the bottom of ships. Since then it has multiplied uncontrollably, and vast areas of rock, once occupied by the less aggressive limpets and a wide variety of other intertidal organisms, have been given over to monospecific stands of black mussel. Their range now extends between Hermanus and Port Nolloth on the west coast, and they have been introduced to the shores at Port Elizabeth on the south coast. This species constitutes a serious threat to coastal biodiversity.

In their diversity of form and feature the marine systems abutting the Peninsula are an integral component of the region. From the rocky protrusions of Cape Point in the south, to the sheer cliffs and deep aquamarine waters of Hout Bay in the west, and then to the beaches and sheltered coves on the eastern side of the Peninsula, they are an important ingredient in the magic of the Cape Peninsula. Its various names – Cape of Storms, Cape of Good Hope – aptly fit this rocky promontory: an Eden encompassing mountain peaks, rugged cliffs, wetland seeps, sandy beaches, pounding waves and endless seascapes that merge with the boundaries of the sky.

It has been said that with its Mediterranean climate the Cape Peninsula lacks the element of classical Africa. Yet in its adaptation to adversity – to fire, drought, scorching winds, wet winters, arid summers and a perpetual struggle for nutrients – it foreshadows the conditions of the regions further north. The currents that shape marine faunal communities here play a more fundamental role on the coast of Namaqualand; the vegetation adapted to harsh conditions on the Peninsula gives way to a floral community that takes adaptation to adversity to new heights; the watery seeps of the Peninsula are represented further north by short-lived ephemeral pools. These Edens are bound together by their almost untouched biotas, their unique landscapes, and their vulnerability to human development.

OPPOSITE: *At times, the west coast is transformed by violent waves that thunder up its beaches and across its rocky shores.*
ABOVE LEFT: *Long sandy beaches stretch for kilometres along parts of the west coast.*
ABOVE CENTRE: *Sparse dune vegetation clings onto the wind-rippled sand.*
ABOVE RIGHT: *Exposed layers of granite, Table Mountain sandstone and shales at Chapman's Peak bear witness to the geological history of the Peninsula.*
LEFT: *A kelp gull soars over foam-crested waves near Cape Point.*

It is said of people who move to Namaqualand that
they only cry twice: once when they arrive, and once
when they leave. It is a saying that epitomises the land
– a strip no more than 150 kilometres wide that
extends up the west coast of South Africa,
and into southern Namibia.

The Orange River coursing through the Richtersveld.

Namaqua daisies in spring.

Delicate dune vegetation.

Namaqualand

GARDEN OF FLOWERING STONES

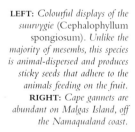

LEFT: *Colourful displays of the suurvygie* (Cephalophyllum spongiosum). *Unlike the majority of mesembs, this species is animal-dispersed and produces sticky seeds that adhere to the animals feeding on the fruit.*
RIGHT: *Cape gannets are abundant on Malgas Island, off the Namaqualand coast.*

Bisected by a green belt of vegetation that marks the Orange River on the border between Namibia and South Africa, the area known as Namaqualand is an otherwise barren, unforgiving territory. One early European settler described it thus: "as dry as a plank and ... nothing but sand dotted with molehills. There is neither foliage nor grass there, nothing but an occasional puddle of muddy water, so brackish that its edges are encrusted with salt". By contrast, other travellers to the region exulted: "the whole country affords a fine field for botany, being enamelled with the greatest number of flowers I ever saw, of exquisite beauty and fragrance".

This is Namaqualand, a land whose bleak greyness is interspersed by periods of lush greenery after the brief winter rains; a terrain both forbidding, yet embracing; harsh, yet delicate in spring; barren, but rich in diversity. In terms of vegetation, the area supports what is technically known as the "succulent karoo biome" – a diverse array of unique flora, adapted to survival in this harsh land of low rainfall, scorching summer temperatures, wind-blasted rock faces and scouring sands. It is also a land of intricate adaptations where microhabitat intrigues more than the landscape. Thus while it is no place for the well-intentioned safari traveller, with a tick-list of big game to cross off, if one takes time to stop and bend low over the grey stones and the bleached thorny scrub, an astounding variety of plant and animal life becomes apparent.

Land of contrasts

Bounded in the south by the Olifants River and in the north by the sand dunes of the Namib Desert, Namaqualand encompasses a number of unique areas. These include the Sperrgebiet of southern Namibia and the massive rock formations of the Richtersveld – a barren mountainous wilderness whose aridity contrasts with the dark green belt of the Orange River that meanders slowly between the mountains. Further south, and again in complete contrast to the awe-inspiring ranges of the Richtersveld, are the gently undulating, pebble-strewn plains of the Knersvlakte, so named, apparently, after the chattering of teeth engendered by a wagon ride through the area.

Moving west across Namaqualand, one first traverses the Hardeveld, a rolling mass of granite domes, "klipkoppies" (stony hills) and rocky slopes. This region receives marginally more rainfall than the surrounding veld of Namaqualand and as a result has a soft green tinge of vegetation, even during the hottest months of summer. The Hardeveld zone extends westward to within about 30 kilometres of the sea, whereupon the terrain changes again, passing into the coastal Sandveld zone.

This zone stretches along the coast from the Olifants River in the south to the Orange River, and comprises mainly low-growing shrubs, scattered across the shallow Namaqua sands. On the coast itself, the land gives way to long, sandy beaches and formidable rocky shores, bathed by the icy waters of the Atlantic Ocean and the Benguela current.

It is this current that plays a fundamental role in determining the climate of Namaqualand – the backdrop against which all else must function. Its surface waters the result of upwelling water from the icy ocean depths, the Benguela current is extremely cold and the cold air above holds little water vapour. As a result, air moving in towards the land results in thick fogs but little rain, thus accounting for the general aridity of these coastal lands.

Rainfall here is therefore scarce and highly seasonal, with the region receiving, at best, 300 millimetres during the winter wet season. Thus the fogs that move inland, particularly during hot summer evenings, provide a grudging but vital source of water that is essential to the survival of the Namaqualand flora and fauna – a resource that many of these organisms have developed intriguing mechanisms to exploit in their struggle for survival.

The marine realm

While the Benguela current offers only scant resources to the parched land, it confers a bounteous supply of nutrients to the marine biota. This is due to a process known as upwelling, brought about by the action of strong south-easterly winds, blowing in the same direction as the icy Benguela. As the winds blow, surface waters are pushed ahead of them, and deflected offshore. Cold waters from deeper down rise up to take their place on the surface, bringing with them a rich supply of nutrients, accumulated on the ocean floor. These nutrients, absorbed by plants that form the base of the marine food chain, account for the phenomenally high biomass occurring within the marine ecosystems, which contrasts so strongly with the bleak aridity of the surrounding land.

The marine plantlife immediately off the west coast of southern Africa has the luxuriant appearance of dense stands of tropical forest. Forests of kelp, *Laminaria pallida*, grow in a wide band in the rocky reefs of the shallow subtidal, accompanied by a range of green, brown and red seaweeds. The kelp beds serve as habitat for a wide array of marine life, including sea urchins, alikreukel and the scavenging west-coast rock lobster, *Jasus lalandii*, an important resource for west-coast fisheries. In the intertidal zone of the rocky shores, the pounding waves bring with them minute particles of organic material, providing a food source for the densely packed layers of filter feeders, such as the Cape reef worm, *Gunnarea capensis*, and mussels, including the invasive alien species *Mytilus galloprovincialis*.

The rocky shores also support the highest biomass of intertidal grazers found anywhere in the world. Large, dome-shaped *Patella argenvillei* limpets dominate the lower intertidal, feeding on kelp fronds, which they trap by clamping down their shells. In more sheltered bays, *Patella granatina* limpets feed in a similar manner, while higher up the shore *Patella granularis* limpets move over the rock surfaces, grazing on microalgal growths. In the past, these rich marine resources were heavily utilised by nomadic groups of Stone Age man, known locally as *strandlopers* (beach walkers). Today, heaps of fossil middens are still in evidence among the high-shore rocks and dunes, where thousands of mussel and limpet shells lie piled – scant remains of a previous people's struggle for survival in this land.

The black masses of dolomite comprising the rocky shores of the west coast are separated by long expanses of wave-washed sand. These beaches are inhabited by a number of organisms, finely attuned to utilise whatever produce the sea casts up. Of these, the giant isopod *Tylos granulatus* is perhaps the most endearing. These creatures, measuring up to two centimetres in length, spend their days in burrows above the high water mark of the tide. At night they emerge in their hundreds, their dark eyes glittering against the white plates of their armouring, to scavenge on pieces of rotting kelp or dead animals deposited by the tide.

ABOVE: *Sunset softens a deserted Namaqualand beach.*
FAR LEFT: *Grey herons shrouded in early morning fog.*
CENTRE: *On the low-shore, the kelp-trapping* Patella argenvillei *limpets attain high densities.*
LEFT: Patella argenvillei *(top) and* P. cochlear *(bottom) occur in distinct zonations on the rocky shore.*

Offshore, the nutrient-rich waters of the Benguela nourish dense blooms of tiny plant cells called phytoplankton. These in turn support minute animals, known as zooplankton, which thrive on the phytoplankton. In turn the zooplankton are fed on by larger predators, thus accounting finally for the rich fish resources off the west coast. With such a plentiful supply of seafood, it is of little surprise that the Namaqualand coast is also home to a multitude of birds, as well as the Cape fur seal (*Arctocephalus pusillus*). Birds such as penguins, cormorants and gannets nest in colonies on the small islands near to the coast, where their young are protected from predators. Seals, their numbers decimated in the past by sealing activities, now breed in huge colonies along the coast. Looking out to sea, Heaviside's dolphins (*Cephalorhynchus heavisidii*) are also a common sight, their lithe bodies cutting cleanly through the white-capped waves.

The Namaqualand flora

Set against the backdrop of glittering blue seas and abundant marine life, the habitual grey scrubby vegetation of the succulent karoo stands out in stark contrast. On land, plant survival is enabled only by an intriguing array of adaptations, allowing organisms to withstand the heat, cold, aridity, winds and harsh surroundings. Thus, most plants here are low-growing shrubs – an adaptation that allows them to escape blasting by the winds – and trees in the succulent karoo are rare.

As its name suggests, the flora of the succulent karoo comprises mainly succulents – plants with fleshy, waterproof leaves and stems that are able to store water over long periods of time. Rainfall is too low, and conditions in general too harsh, for grasses to survive and they are thus rare. Even succulents are not able to withstand years of drought, however, and they rely on regular, if low, contributions of rainfall and dew precipitated from fogs. This restricts their range to the succulent karoo areas rather than the less predictable Kalahari. In the south of Namaqualand, precipitation occurs primarily during winter. Further north, however, and inland, this pattern is tempered by summer rainfall areas in the east, where rain falls during both winter and summer. The plants grow in soils that are for the most part rich in lime, but shallow, and prone to erosion both by the scouring south-easterly winds and the hot, dry "berg" winds that blow in from the east.

Perhaps the best known of all succulents are those of the family Mesembryanthemoideae, more commonly called "mesembs". With approximately 2 500 different species comprising the family, an estimated 92 per cent of which are endemic to the succulent karoo, this family is the largest in southern Africa, and emphasises the importance of this unlikely-looking scrubland in terms of floral biodiversity. Mesembs encompass a broad range of sizes and forms, from the small, pebble-like *Lithops* plants, to dwarf shrubs. Almost all mesembs produce brightly coloured flowers that, after the winter rains, give rise to spectacular displays of colour across the sandy veld.

Aside from succulents, other important flora include geophytes – plants that store water below the ground, in large bulbs or tubers. These plants remain dormant during the hot dry season, the bulbs insulated to some extent by the overlying sand. After the first rains have fallen, however, the bulbs sprout and produce leaves, using stored food and water to promote this initial surge of growth.

Whereas geophytes conserve water by burying their tubers beneath the ground, succulents such as the stone plants (*Lithops*) take adaptation to an extreme, and the whole leaf is buried beneath the soil, with only the flattened tips sticking above the ground, like a small pebble. This adaptation does however have a downside, in that exposure to light, necessary for the energy-producing process

OPPOSITE: *During periods of lower sunlight, when insect numbers are reduced, mesemb flowers partially close, only opening in bright sunlight, when insect numbers are high. In this way the plant is able to tailor distribution of nectar resources to periods when they will be most utilised.*
ABOVE LEFT: *A yellow cluster of* Didelta sp. *in a sea of purple.*
ABOVE RIGHT: *Detail of the tiny* Lithops.
LEFT: *Clusters of* Lithops *camouflaged on a gravel bed.*
RIGHT: *Lichen fields near Alexander Bay.*

of photosynthesis, is thereby reduced. In many plants, including *Lithops*, this problem has been averted by the evolution of small translucent "windows" on the exposed leaf tips, which allow light to pass down to green, photosynthesising cells far below. This adaptation has led to such plants being named *Fensterpflanzen*, or window plants.

Many other superb adaptations to survival are displayed by the flora occupying the harsh climes of Namaqualand, where the ability to conserve water assumes an overriding priority. Succulents have large storage organs in the form of their swollen leaves and stems, but these would be of little avail if they allowed water to evaporate out of their leaves into the dry air outside. Waterproofing of the plant has thus been developed, through the secretion of waxy layers on the plant's outer surface, the layer usually increasing in thickness during summer. Another way of decreasing loss of water from plant surfaces is to decrease the amount of area exposed to the air. Thus many of the plants of this biome have small leaves, covered with a tough waxy layer, while others, such as the delicate uintjie (*Moraea tortilis*) twist their leaves into a fine corkscrew, to reduce the amount of surface exposed to sun and wind, and thus to evaporation.

Not all plants follow these rules, however. The broad leaves of the suikerkannetjie (*Massonia depressa*), for example, extend out across the ground, apparently in defiance of the need to reduce loss of water from their surfaces. Closer investigation has revealed, however, that these plants probably achieve even greater feats of water conservation by covering the ground overlying their bulbs, thus protecting these vital storage organs from desiccation. In addition, their large leaves, located close to the ground, play an important role in trapping water. During the night, the thick fogs that roll in from the sea condense on the leaves, and precious drops of water collect at the base of the plant. The fogs play a vital role in the survival of the succulent karoo flora, some of which are capable of absorbing water vapour through small one-way valve systems located on their leaves.

The moist fogs are also utilised by lichens, another component of this strange and diverse community. In contrast to most plants of the succulent karoo, lichens have evolved no adaptations towards restricting the passage of water across their surfaces, or thalli. They are thus prone to rapid desiccation, but are nevertheless able to withstand water loss, often over long periods of time. After rainfall, or at night, if a fog bank moves in, the dry, shrivelled thalli unfold and absorb water rapidly. In the early morning light, for a brief while until desiccation sets in once more, they are able to photosynthesise freely.

Lichens are an intriguing community. Each lichen comprises a combination of fungi and algae in a symbiotic relationship, the fungi supplying the physical support for the organism, while the algae provides food and energy through photosynthesis. In the succulent karoo, many lichens grow on dead plants and rocks, their long dry thalli hanging down in wispy strands. Others are found beneath small translucent quartz pebbles. Fog condenses on the cool pebbles at night, supplying sufficient moisture for the lichen's survival, and leading to the formation of areas of orange-hued pebble fields.

Flora versus fauna

While conservation of water is probably most vital to a plant's survival in Namaqualand, the loss of body tissue to herbivores entails serious, and sometimes fatal, costs to the plant. In this arid climate, the loss of even tiny leaves represents a substantial waste of stored water or hard-won energy. To counteract such losses, many plant species have invested energy in the evolution of defence mechanisms to discourage grazers. Thorns, tannins and even toxins are just some examples of the strategies implemented.

Among the geophytes, the use of toxins is well developed, because they are highly vulnerable to grazing and nibbling. Their new shoots are often the first to appear in spring, after a long season when grazing is limited. By the time these shoots emerge, grazers are eager for any green material. To make matters worse, many geophytes produce only a single stem. If this is consumed, the plant loses its only means of replenishing its energy stores. The tubers of geophytes are also often under siege. During the dry season, they constitute an important source of nutrition and water for many animals. Indeed, they are almost the staple diet of several subterranean animals, including the Namaqua dune molerat.

In the light of the gravity of tubers being consumed, it is not surprising that many geophytes do possess toxic compounds. Thus tubers of members of the family Iridaceae are all highly toxic, and responsible for the fatal "tulp" poisoning that afflicts stock in the farming lands of the succulent karoo. The common chincherinchee (*Ornithogalum* spp.) is also highly poisonous, and consumption of the flowers can be fatal.

Although several species of relatively large browsers are found in Namaqualand, including springbok *(Antidorcas marsupialis)* and the shy steenbok *(Raphicerus campestris)* – a selective browser that supplements its diet by scraping up underground tubers – the majority of herbivores found here are insects. These in turn are preyed upon by a variety of other animals. Reptiles are particularly well adapted to life in this wilderness, and of the 45 species of reptile found in Namaqualand, 19 are endemic to the succulent karoo. One of these is the smallest of the African adders, the Namaqua dwarf adder (*Bitis schneideri*), measuring only 20 to 25 centimetres in length. Frogs also contribute to vertebrate diversity, and the small, soft, unlikely-looking rain frogs (species of the genus *Breviceps*), which emerge from underground refugia only after rain, heighten the contrast between the moist spring and the arid summer.

For most of the animals of Namaqualand, the struggle for survival is a hard one, involving coping with long periods during which food is in short supply. Many species have had to make an evolutionary choice between the advantages of being solitary and coming into contact with other members of the species only for brief periods to breed, versus the advantages of group or colonial living. Wasps are amongst those that have taken the former route, finding enough pollen and food material to sustain individuals throughout the year, but not enough to support whole hives.

One solution to the problem of ensuring that an animal has food supplies for the entire year is to accumulate it when it is most abundant, and use this store to tide the animal over the long dry season. Molerats have perfected this art. The solitary Namaqua dune molerat (*Bathyergus janetta*) stores bulbs and tubers in a small "pantry" section of its underground burrow. The bulbs are well-maintained – any signs of sprouting are at once curtailed by nipping off the shoot as it appears. The stored food is particularly important during the breeding season. After giving birth to a litter of young, the female lives off her store, reducing the amount of energy-taxing foraging that would otherwise be necessary.

While wasps and Namaqua dune molerats have adopted a solitary existence, other species have found more success in co-operative living. Suricates (*Suricata suricatta*), for example, live in colonies of up to 30 individuals. For these animals, the principal advantage of living in a group lies in predator avoidance. Suricates primarily eat small insects, which they find by digging into burrows and scratching away at the hard soil. This means that while they are feeding, with their eyes and noses in the ground, they are highly vulnerable to predators. Birds of prey, including the large martial eagle (*Polemaetus bellicosus*), black-backed jackals (*Canis mesomelas*) and snakes are common predators in the succulent karoo. Suricate

colonies thus post sentries, usually sub-adults, that guard against predators while the rest of the colony feeds. When danger approaches, the guards emit a shrill sound that alerts the group.

Such social living also entails other advantages for the suricates. Each colony has a dominant female, which is usually the only breeder in the colony. When a litter is produced, sub-adult females are used as "baby-sitters" and remain at the nest site, while the mother goes out and forages. Since members of the same colony are related, all gain from this system: sub-adult sentries and baby-sitters are contributing to the survival of their close relatives, and thus ensuring the continuation of their own genetic line.

Group living is not confined to the hunted. Brown hyaenas, which scrape a part-scavenging, part-hunting existence from the succulent karoo, also live in small groups. They are found throughout the succulent karoo and the Kalahari, scavenging on dead animals such as seal pups that wash up on the coast, as well as hunting for occasional smaller prey. When a female in the group has pups, roaming males bring food back to the den, thereby reducing the amount of foraging which she would have had to do if left alone, and thus indirectly increasing the number of times when she can breed. In the den, females care for the young of the group and indeed even allow the cubs of other females to suckle. Such co-operative behaviour is again to the advantage of all, since through assisting in the survival of young of the group, members increase the survival of their own genetic line, albeit not a direct line.

The Garden of Eden

For most animals and plants of Namaqualand, the annual cycle involves adopting a technique that will allow the organism to survive the long, dry months of summer, sometimes even in a state of diapause or hibernation. This enables it to take

LEFT: *A cricket* (Hetrodes pupa) *makes the most of the abundant supplies of pollen in spring.*
ABOVE: *The sharp spines of the sweet doringbos* (Cordon royonii) *protect it from grazers.*
ABOVE RIGHT: *Open flowers of a* Hoodia *plant emit the smell of rotting meat to attract pollinating flies.*
RIGHT: *The pied kingfisher is a common resident of west coast estuaries.*

advantage of the brief respite offered by the winter rains, to grow and reproduce. Thus, for the greater part of the year, the terrain is, from a distance, bleak, grey-brown and apparently devoid of life, and it is only close up, or during the cooler silences of the night, that the diversity of life forms comprising this unique ecosystem become apparent.

Towards the end of winter, however, when the soft grey winter rains have sunk into the parched sands, Namaqualand undergoes a spectacular transformation. Almost overnight, the landscape changes from drab grey-browns to greens. Dry river beds, unrecognisable as such in summer save for the tell-tale signs of the *Acacia karoo* and camelthorn trees that line their courses, become first sandy trickles, then swirling muddy waters that surge along their shallow channels.

There are few perennial rivers in Namaqualand, other than the Orange and Olifants rivers. For the rest, they are highly seasonal, flowing only for brief periods during the rainy season and even then, seldom breaking through their estu-

ary mouths and opening into the sea. Instead, most lose momentum as they reach the coast, and sink slowly into the loose sands. Only after exceptionally high rainfall do the rivers succeed in mounting the slowly accumulated sand banks lying between the river and the sea. These rare occasions are probably of immense ecological importance, allowing accumulated salts to be flushed from the estuary and aquatic animals to move between the estuary and the sea.

Some time after the rains, spring comes to Namaqualand. It arrives suddenly, taking the rain-softened land by surprise. Within days of the first shy blooms appearing, the once barren landscape erupts in a mass of colour, flowers opening in quick succession like cooking popcorn. Even in the splendour of the spring flowers, however, there is a sense of urgency, a need to take full advantage of the brief interlude when the ground is soft and moisture-laden, and the sun, though always warm, does not scorch. Whereas in other less harsh biomes, different species of plants are able to spread out their flowering seasons, thus reducing

CIRCLES IN THE SAND

Looking out across the flat Namaqua earth and onto the gentle slopes of the low hills, a curious phenomenon comes into view. Overlaid on the grey-brown vegetation are circles of darker plants, regularly spaced, and, on closer inspection, slightly raised. During the spring flowering season, these round circles or *heuweltjies* as they are called in South Africa, are still more prominent, and it becomes obvious, even from a distance, that the plant species existing inside the circles are different to those growing on the surrounding veld.

Known as "fairy rings" in Namibia, and once believed to be the work of mystical creatures, the origin of *heuweltjies* was long the subject of considerable debate, even amongst those who, sadly, have discarded the notion of fairy creators. Today, however, it seems certain that the existence of *heuweltjies* is due primarily to the ancient activities of termites, and that the raised circles are the remnants of their mounds. These origins are fascinating, in that they highlight the remarkable effect of termites on soil structure, to the extent that they alter plant communities and create small terrestrial "islands" of biodiversity.

During mound construction, termites process grains of soil, using saliva and a material called calcrete to bind the soil together. When these mounds eventually break down, the soil remaining is finer and more alkaline than that in the surrounding areas, resulting in differences in both chemistry and water retention. Plants that grow in the *heuweltjies* tend to favour wetter soils, while vegetation in the surrounding areas is adapted to dry, sandy soils, and fails to establish itself within the termite zones. The result is a bizarre segregation of habitats and communities, bearing testimony to the phenomenal land-forming activities of creatures no bigger than a few millimetres in length.

BELOW: *Heuweltjies show up as small circles against the dry Richtersveld terrain.*

competition for pollinators and dispersers, the flowering season in Namaqualand is too short to allow for this luxury. Thus thousands of species all bloom within a few weeks of each other, and it is this factor that largely accounts for the extraordinary diversity of shape, colour, fragrance and distribution used by different species to attract pollinators.

The first problem facing a flowering plant is the need for an energetically inexpensive yet efficient means of being pollinated. On a superficial level, it seems obvious that wind pollination is the cheapest method, since complex systems of rewarding the pollinator for its efforts, such as by the provision of pollen or nectar to the pollinator, are rendered unnecessary. However, in a terrain such as Namaqualand where plants in general are sparse, and plants of the same species still more so, or alternatively, are clustered in isolated, small groups, successful wind pollination would necessitate generating huge volumes of pollen, at the cost of valuable energy, to ensure that at least some reached its rightful location. Thus most plants have opted for a more specialised approach to pollination, primarily making use of insects.

Insects are ideal pollinators of plants from this region, in that not only can different insects be selectively attracted to different plant species, but their own life cycles are short enough to be synchronised with the flowering times of plants. Many insects go into states of diapause, pupate or survive as eggs during the dry season, emerging only when conditions are favourable. Such a mechanism bypasses the plant's problem of having to maintain a source of living pollinators throughout the year when resources are limited, merely so that they will be present during the short season when resources are abundant. Some insects, such as honey bees, cannot enter diapause, and thus play a minor role in the pollination of Namaqualand's blooms.

When the flowers of Namaqualand do open, competition for pollinators is intense. Each plant is in a race against time: it must be pollinated, produce seeds, mature and finally disperse the seeds, all during the few short weeks when conditions are favourable, before Namaqualand returns to its hot and arid summertime norm. This then accounts for the variety of colours displayed by Namaqualand's flora, and the spectacular springtime displays that each year draw thousands of visitors to this unique wilderness.

Some flowers are particularly well adapted to attracting pollinators. Members of the Asteraceae (daisy) family, for example, have highly complex flowers, each so-called "flower-head" consisting, in reality, of a multitude of tiny coloured flowers, with "ray florets", around the perimeter of a mass of smaller "disc florets". Since each floret has its own supply of nectar, an insect visiting a single plant is rewarded with a large total nectar supply. The insect lands on a ray and walks

ABOVE: *The bark of the bastard quiver tree is adapted to reflect heat off the plant.*
RIGHT: *Roots of the shepherd's tree, also known as the "tree of life" because of the shade it produces, twist their way through a giant boulder.*

towards the centre, rubbing pollen from other flower heads onto the stigmas of the florets as it does so. In this manner, large numbers of florets can be fertilised in quick succession and many seeds thus produced.

This is particularly important for plants such as the Asteraceae. Not only are large numbers of seeds doomed, but because Asteraceae are annuals, unlike succulents, each plant has only one chance at producing seeds. This short life-cycle has its advantages. For one thing, the plants do not have to invest in energy-taxing mechanisms for protection against desiccation. Instead, their stems and leaves are soft, and they have no need of thorns. On the other hand, if the flowers are not pollinated during its single growing season, the plant will not have succeeded in passing its genetic material on to a new generation. A plentiful supply of seeds is thus vital.

It is all very well for plants to produce large numbers of seed, but ensuring that these seeds will actually survive and grow is another matter altogether, and has been approached by different plants in a variety of ways.

The first dilemma surrounding the notion of dispersal is how far away to disperse the seeds. In Namaqualand, wind dispersal is the most frequent method of dispersal, and most seeds are light, and often equipped with hairs, "wings" or other structures aimed at controlling the distances to which the wind will carry them. If seeds are scattered far away, and survive, then the plant will have colonised new areas. There are no guarantees, however, that the seeds will in fact land in areas that are suitable for growth. Thus a safer option for the plant might be to drop its seeds nearby, where conditions have already been proven to be suitable for growth of the species. In the case of the Asteraceae, both these methods are adopted, with flowers producing a combination of seed types.

The succulent mesembs have evolved a particularly ingenious method of seed dispersal. While annuals have to disperse their seeds at the end of spring, when the parent plant dies, perennials such as the succulents do not have this constant pressure. The seeds are thus retained in a woody capsule, sealed by valves. When the valves are wet, they open and, if the capsule is shaken by raindrops, the seeds are released. As the valves dry out, they close again. The plant thus helps to ensure that its seeds are released when conditions for germination are most favourable.

Given the great variety of mesembs within Namaqualand, it is not however surprising that they should display a similar diversity in the mechanisms by which their capsule systems operate. While some plants forcibly catapult their seeds out of the capsule after a wetting, others, such as the tiny, ground-hugging *Lithops*, allow their capsules to fill with water collecting on the ground, and the seeds to be thus flushed out of the capsule. This is a particularly ingenious method for dispersing such plants that inhabit tiny cracks, as the seeds, washing gently over the rocks, are likely to lodge in similar cracks.

The Richtersveld

Whereas the displays of spring flowers in the flat stretches of sandveld are spectacular, it is in the bleak splendour of the Richtersveld that they are truly awesome, the annuals transforming barren gravel sands to waving seas of colour, while the succulents bloom in isolated beauty from cracks in seemingly inhospitable boulder formations.

The harsh beauty of the Richtersveld is like no other part of Namaqualand. Bleak and savage in summer, strangely softened by flowers and greenery in spring, its mountain formations bear testimony to a tumultuous past. Huge granite boulders, once flung angrily from the bowels of the earth, now lie piled in savage splendour. In the east, the granite mountains are streaked with harsh black dolomite and veins of white quartz. Below, the stony valleys open into gravel plains. With summertime temperatures reaching 50 °C and rain falling sometimes not at all, at other times in violent thunderstorms that quickly swell the desolate river beds, it is not a land for the faint-hearted.

In such a moonscape of sun-baked rocks and succulents, the bizarre sight of a halfmens (*Pachypodium namaquanum*) seems hardly unexpected. This strange tree, one of the few trees found in the succulent karoo, and endemic to the Richtersveld, is according to local legend half man and half plant, created when members of some ancient tribe were exiled from their people in the north and turned into trees. From their rocky perches in the Richtersveld, they turn their heads perpetually towards the north from whence they came. Indeed, the halfmens do point their heads towards the north, although a more mundane explanation is that this is in order to protect the delicate growing tips of their leaves from the harsh sun, which shines from the north for the greater part of the year. Bent at an angle towards the sun, a shield of older leaves on the apex of the stalk shades the young leaf tips.

Two other trees are endemic to this area: the bastard quiver tree (*Aloe pillansii*) and the maiden's quiver tree (*Aloe ramosissima*). These trees are able to survive on the rocky mountains and the gravel plains of the Richtersveld and provide some of the only sources of wood away from the water courses to which more common trees such as the sweet thorn (*Acacia karoo*) are restricted. This property made them valuable to local people, and the San or Bushmen, for example, used the hollowed-out wood to make quivers for their arrows.

Even the rivers in the Richtersveld are dry beds of rock and gravel for most of the year, transforming themselves only now and again into short-lived torrents of water. The exception to this is the Orange River, which, like some dryland deity, passes unscathed between the tortured mountains, its banks defining a dark green swathe of life and water against the shimmering black rocks. This great river

FAR LEFT: *In the Richtersveld, granite boulders, bubbled up from the depths of the earth aeons earlier, lie scattered over the surface.*
LEFT: *The curious halfmens trees of the Richtersveld.*

is of immense importance to life in the Richtersveld. Its broad valley funnels the moist fogs that roll in from the sea, bringing precious moisture far inland. Being a perennial system, its waters also provide a longitudinal oasis in the bleak surrounds, providing habitat for such unexpected animals as the Cape clawless otter (*Aonyx capensis*) and the water monitor (*Varanus niloticus*). At the river mouth, the banks widen and give rise to a large wetland system, which is of significant value as a breeding and feeding ground for many species of birds, and, as such, has worldwide recognition as an important wetland.

Ironically, while the waters of the Orange River provide life to the Namaqualand flora and fauna, they also brought with them long ago the seeds of its destruction, in the form of a rich harvest of alluvial diamonds. Originating in kimberlite pipes far inland, the diamonds have been slowly eroded out of their settings, and washed downstream. As the river sweeps out to sea, it meets the north-flowing streams of the Benguela current, and its load of silt, gravel and diamonds are swept along with the current, and dropped out of the water column some distance out to sea, and along the coast. Today, alluvial diamonds are mined from the Orange River, the surrounding floodplain, from deposits in the sea itself and along the coast where the sea once extended and dropped its precious load on what is now dry land. Large areas of Namaqualand have been scarred by these old mines, which dug and sifted through the once succulent-rich sands, leaving behind areas of land covered only by small mounds of discarded overburden or massive dunes of processed sand. Fortunately, since then, changes in legislation require rehabilitation to take place, and new mining works leave little of the desolation of their predecessors.

The Sperrgebiet

In the Sperrgebiet the struggle between man and the barren forces of the Namaqualand wilderness seem most evident. The name means "forbidden territory", reflecting both its status as a high-security, restricted diamond mining area and possibly the way early settlers would have regarded the terrain. Here, on the borders of Namaqualand, the fragility of the semi-desert system is emphasised by the well-preserved reminders of man's ravages. Ghost mining towns, abandoned during the early part of this century as local diamond supplies dwindled, loom strangely across the wind-swept plains. Blasted by sands, and corroded by sea air, the overriding dryness of the climate has nevertheless preserved much of the original structure of these towns, in an eerie frieze of history. Today, the ghost towns are inhabited largely by solitary brown hyaenas and black-backed jackals that scavenge along the coast for pickings, moving inland during the wetter spring to plunder nests and feast on small rodents. Despite the scarring wreaked by the quest for diamonds, the Sperrgebiet remains an area of dramatic rock formations, sand dunes, gravel plains and salt-encrusted ephemeral pans.

Namaqualand. Land of contrasts, where mere survival deserves acclaim, but where the very harshness of the terrain renders it more fragile, less able to cover its man-inflicted wounds with a thick bandage of hide-all vegetation. Too small a desert to repel man altogether, but too barren a wilderness to be able to accommodate him, this Eden seems ever more vulnerable, its landscape more precious than the diamonds that it yields.

MASTERS OF THE WEST COAST FISHERIES

On small islands off the coast of Namaqualand, pairs of Cape gannets (*Morus capensis*) nest beak by jowl in their hundreds in the thick bed of guano (bird faeces) covering the island. This guano, the accumulation of generations of bird faeces, rich in phosphorus, was once eagerly sought for use in commercial fertilisers. In fact, so desirable was the "white gold" that battles were fought over it and gunships were despatched to establish territorial rights. In time, whole islands were denuded of their pungent cover, and nest sites destroyed.

Guano is an important symbol of, and contributor to, the productivity of the marine ecosystems around the west coast. Run-off from the bird colonies on islands leads to rich soupy bands of organic material around the island perimeters, resulting in massive algal production, which in turn yields high biomasses of limpets on the rocky intertidal shores of the islands. Such proliferation of marine resources supports large numbers of avian predators, such as the African black oystercatcher (*Haematopus moquini*), which thrive in this area from where their own predators are excluded.

The guano itself is the product of the same productive ecosystem to which it contributes. In the Benguela ecosystem, fish resources are particularly rich, due to the phenomenon of upwelling. Gannets feed mainly on fish, and are remarkably adapted to fishing on the wing. Their eyesight is highly developed to enable accurate dives on fish below, while their skulls are equipped with a system of air sacs to cushion the brain against the impact of these high-speed dives into the water. Much maligned for their apparently graceless lift-offs into the air, gannets are masters of the sky. Their large wingspans (up to two metres) give them considerable power, while the accuracy of their dives is honed by the use of their tail as a rudder, steering the bird as it plummets down through the air.

Gannets nest in large colonies on the small islands off the west coast of southern Africa, spending most of their lives fishing at sea. Since gannets nest on the ground they are extremely vulnerable to predation and these islands, inaccessible to territorial predators, are the perfect habitat. The nests consist of shallow depressions scooped out of the thick layers of accumulated guano. Here, carefully positioned out of beak range of the jostling neighbours, pairs of gannets raise a single chick, one bird staying with the offspring while the other flies off in search of food.

Given the density and apparent confusion of the gannet colonies, it seems highly unlikely that gannet parents, leaving the nest to catch food, should have any chance at all of finding it again. Incredibly, they do so, circling several times over the colony while they home in on the exact nest location, and then dropping down into it with great precision. Once safely landed, the gannet engages in an elaborate recognition ritual with its mate, the two birds intertwining their necks, and crossing their beaks.

BELOW: *To the casual observer, a gannet breeding colony is a mêlée of squawking, flapping, pecking birds. Despite appearances, however, gannets have developed a highly complex system of behavioural signals, to reduce the inevitable aggression that must result from large numbers of birds breeding in such close proximity.*

CHAPTER 3

*A belt of ancient, wind-blown sands, held together by sparse,
arid-adapted vegetation, extends from the southern part of the
Democratic Republic of Congo, as far south as the northern
Cape of South Africa, forming in its more desolate expanses an
Eden still too harsh to be tamed, as yet too arid to be spoiled, a land
rich in diamonds but where water is the most precious commodity.*

The first raindrops of the season fall on the red Kalahari sands.

Zebra skeleton on Makgadikgadi Pan.

Drotsky's Cave.

THE *Kalahari*

DRYLANDS OF SOUTHERN AFRICA

LEFT: *A camelthorn tree, symbol
of the Kalahari, breaks the flat
aridity of the landscape.*
RIGHT: *Suricate on sentry duty.*

Commonly referred to as a desert, due to the paucity of its surface waters, the Kalahari is in fact primarily a semi-arid area, its vast, seemingly barren landscape sparsely covered by what is formally known as arid savannah vegetation. It is also home to a surprisingly large variety of animals, each either uniquely adapted to survival in this bleak terrain, or using it transiently during brief episodes of plenty. Only in the far south, where the red sand dunes of the Northern Cape appear, can the Kalahari truly be termed a desert.

The rest of the Kalahari is a wide, flat expanse of sand, scantily covered by small shrubs and sun-whitened grasses. Occasional stands of trees form woodland patches, or line the courses of dry river beds. In northern Botswana, the rocky outcrops of the Tsodilo Hills provide some relief to the rolling monotony of the landscape, while further east the Makgadikgadi Pans, relics of a bygone age when vast areas of the Kalahari were covered by an immense inland lake, stretch across the landscape, their surfaces cracked and dry for much of the year.

Up to 500 millimetres of rain fall in the Kalahari each year, but its distribution and timing are unpredictable, and what does fall is quickly absorbed into the deep, thirsty sands. In general, precipitation decreases towards the south, a gradient that is also reflected in the pattern of rivers dissecting the great sandy plains. In the north, three large perennial rivers, the Chobe, Zambezi and Okavango, provide year-long relief to the parched surroundings, the Okavango spreading out across the sands of northern Botswana to form a huge inland delta and wetland paradise. Further south, by

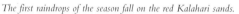

contrast, the Molopo, Auob and Nossob Rivers lie dry and empty for months on end and sometimes even for years, their dry sand and gravel beds changing only occasionally to torrents of debris-ridden muddy water, after brief episodes of heavy rainfall.

Formation of a wilderness

The Kalahari comprises a huge, sand-filled basin, occupying some 2 500 square kilometres of southern Africa. Its formation involved a series of tectonic upheavals, followed by millions of years of erosion and accumulation of sediments. High-lying areas of land were worn away, while depressions silted up, leading at last to the flat, sandy vastness that is characteristic of the Kalahari today. Changes in climate led to steadily increasing aridity in the region, resulting in a proliferation of the arid-adapted plants that are now prevalent.

The dryness of this part of the southern hemisphere was exacerbated some five million years ago by the final glaciation of the Antarctic continent, while strong winds associated with the increase in aridity spread the Kalahari sands across a wide area. Parallel ridges of east-west running sand dunes were created in the central Kalahari region. Subsequent wetter periods allowed the re-establish-

ment of plants on these dunes and today they remain stabilised by duinriet grasses and stands of camelthorn trees. The dunes are separated by low-lying sandy valleys. Even during the dry season, subterranean water flows deep below the valley surfaces, accessible to the long roots of the camelthorn trees, that can extend as much as 30 metres into the ground.

Lost seas: the Makgadikgadi Pans

The period of intense aridity was followed by episodes of tectonic movement that resulted at last in the ponding back of the waters of the upper Zambezi, Chobe and upper Limpopo Rivers. For a while, these waters formed a vast inland lake, covering between 30 000 and 80 000 square kilometres of an area that includes the present extent of the Kalahari. Today, however, Lakes Ngami and Xau, and the two great ephemeral pans, Ntwetwe and Sowa, are lonely relics of the former superlake, with the latter two comprising the Makgadikgadi Pans.

For the most part, these pans are now dry, their salt-encrusted surfaces overlaying a clay bed that is up to 100 metres deep in places. The areas comprising the pans were probably once the deepest sections of the old superlake – and even today, the summit of Kubu Island on Sowa Pan is marked by a ring of smooth,

BOTTOM LEFT: *Makgadikgadi Pans fill after the summer rains.*
FAR LEFT: *The high rate of evaporation on Makgadikgadi soon changes rainwater into a hyper-saline pan, and foam accumulates at the water's edge.*
LEFT: *Footsteps in the mud show where elephants used this waterhole, before it dried up and they had to move on.*
BELOW: *Highveld gerbils are common Kalahari residents, where they feed on a mixed diet of termites, seeds and grasses.*

water-worn pebbles, a subtle reminder of the days when waves washed across the surface of the inland sea. Kubu Island itself is a raised outcrop of ancient rocks, forming a low island in a sea of white, salt-encrusted clay. Set about with stunted baobab trees, the bleak, salt-stained structure has a Tolkienesque air, lowering over the shimmering clays.

As the waters of the great lake slowly subsided, they grew steadily more saline, until at last only small pools of concentrated salts remained. Today, in the lowest-lying areas, even the ground water is saline. This salinity has had a profound effect on the vegetation in the vicinity, with the few trees that do grow there occurring furthest away from the pans, and only grasses growing down to the pan edges.

In the north-west of Ntwetwe Pan, however, a different pattern of vegetation lingers from the time when the barren wastelands of the salt pans were still a huge lake. Here, groves of sweeping *Hyphaene* palm trees more typical of the Okavango wetlands are scattered incongruously amongst the grasslands, in an area where few other trees are able to survive the saline conditions. The size and weight of their fruit suggest that these palms must be dispersed primarily by elephant. Since elephant are not found in this arid region today, the presence of palms must hark back to former times, when herds of elephant were attracted to the shores of the old lake. The tall palm groves thus bear testimony to the startling changes that have occurred here in the relatively recent past.

Today, the surface of the pans is barren. Nothing grows on the salty clays and what water does collect there is soon absorbed. During a good year, the pans receive water from the Boteti River, the most southerly protrusion of the Okavango Delta, as well as from the Nata River, which drains into the north east of Sowa Pan. For the most part, however, they rely on localised rainfall. When this occurs in sufficient quantity, the pans are miraculously transformed into shallow seas, attracting a rich array of waterfowl from the nearby Okavango, as well as numerous migrant bird species.

The birds feed predominantly on crustaceans, such as the tiny brine shrimps and other animals adapted to survival in the salty, ephemeral waters. During the months or years of drought, the brine shrimp eggs have lain dormant in the salty clays. With these first rains, however, they hatch out into a salty pink crustacean soup that is eagerly consumed by the thronging birds.

Even during the rainy season the water is shallow, seldom reaching depths above 20 centimetres, and is ideal for waders: avocets, black-winged stilts and plovers all congregate around the pan edges. The brine shrimps also form the main diet of flamingos, and around this time tens of thousands of flamingos arrive, coming in great pink-hued flocks to partake of the brief period of abundance. During the wet season, both lesser and greater flamingos (*Phoenicopterus minor* and *P. ruber*) are found in the Makgadikgadi Pans and, in years when the rainfall is particularly high, they breed in isolated, inaccessible areas, their plumages suffused in the deep pinks of their breeding colours.

By the end of summer, the pans are dry and barren again, the hot air shimmers above the salt crusts and it is hard to imagine the brief paroxysm of plenty that has just passed. In the Boteti River, however, some water usually remains, and even when the river itself does not flow, deep pools are interspersed along the stretches of sand. As the surrounding areas dry out, small groups of grazers converge at these oases.

Nxai Pan

To the north of the Makgadikgadi Pans, another cluster of ephemeral pans occurs, also a relic of the ancient lake system. Of these, Nxai Pan is the largest. Although the pans all probably had the same origins, the ones in the vicinity of Nxai are quite different, and instead of the briny wastelands of the Makgadikgadi, the rich, clayey soils of these pans result in a thick covering of sweet grasses. Interspersed on the grasslands are clumps of acacias, such as the umbrella thorn (*Acacia tortilis*), as well as mopane trees (*Colophospermum mopane*).

The grasses here provide grazing material for a rich array of animals and, unusually, both impala and springbok congregate here in herds. Springbok

ABOVE: *The sun sets over a dry Kalahari landscape while clouds massing overhead promise rain.*
LEFT: *Soon after the rain the landscape is transformed, and softened, by delicate spring blooms.*
RIGHT: *The gemsbok is physiologically adapted to withstanding the high day-time temperatures of the Kalahari.*
FAR RIGHT: *Damara molerats (*Cryptomys damarensis*) live in underground colonies, feeding on stored geophyte bulbs.*

(*Antidorcas marsupialis*) feed on the sweet grasses of the pan, while impala (*Aepyceros melampus*) are able to survive by browsing in the surrounding mopane veld and utilising the small areas of permanent water. When the rains come, the dry grasses of the pans are transformed into fresh green shoots, while patches of seasonal wild flowers bloom profusely. Of these, the red hues of the striking *Brunsvigia* lily, or candelabra flower, in particular lend an element of colour that is absent during the long parched months of the dry season.

Adapt or die: life in the Kalahari

Water is the most precious commodity of the dry Kalahari wilderness, and it is symbolic that in Botswana, *pula*, which means rain, is the monetary currency. Indeed, life in the Kalahari revolves around the availability of water, and both plants and animals are finely attuned either to its conservation or to the constant need to locate fresh sources of the precious liquid.

In the central Kalahari, water is only available in the pans and rivers for short periods of time, immediately after the rains. Rainfall is preceded by violent thunderstorms, the huge purple-black clouds building up, then subsiding over the parched earth for a period of days or even weeks before they finally release their promised water. Before the rains come, the Kalahari is dry and grey, its sparse grasses sunbleached, the ground dusty and hard, and most of the palatable vegetation long since consumed.

As the dry season nears its end, the camelthorn tree (*Acacia erioloba*) flowers, its bright clusters of yellow pom-poms providing a welcome relief from the dry monotones of the thirstland. The flowers are followed by the production of large, kidney-shaped pods which house up to 25 seeds each, as well as containing a pulpy material high in nutrients (up to 33 per cent protein). The pods are a valuable source of protein for many Kalahari ungulates, while germination of the seeds is enhanced by being consumed. Each seed is encased in a tough outer layer that enables it to withstand the grinding action of the ungulate's teeth, and the seed cannot germinate while this layer is intact. This safeguards the seeds from germinating too soon, when water conditions are not adequate. Once seeds have been consumed, however, and passed whole into the digestive system of the ungulate, digestive enzymes break down the protective layer. The inner seed passes undamaged out of the animal along with the faeces, and is deposited in a fertile pile of manure. Here, surrounded by moisture and nutrients, its chances of successful development are greatly improved.

With the arrival of the rains, the Kalahari is transformed almost overnight into verdant pastures, and it is difficult to imagine the barren aridity of just a few days previously. New grasses sprout from long-dormant seeds, and a multitude of

tuberous plants push their stems up through the deep sands. These plants, exposed for but a few weeks of each season, and sometimes surviving through years of drought, are superbly adapted both to take advantage of favourable conditions and to escape those they would not be able to survive. The tubers store nutrients and water, allowing the plant to remain alive and dormant underground during the dry season for long periods of time. When the rains come, the tubers provide energy for the initial production of shoots and leaves, promoting rapid growth during the short-lived favourable period. Once above ground, the new leaves begin laying down fresh stores of food for subsequent months of drought, adding new layers to the tuber. It is during this period that these plants produce flowers, and the harsh terrain is softened by the delicate hues of their fragile blooms.

Tubers play an important role in the survival of other desert organisms too. Used by ungulates, rodents, the San people and many other inhabitants of the Kalahari, they provide a precious source of water and nutrition. Some tubers attain considerable sizes: bulbs of the morama plant or gemsbok bean (*Tylosema esculenta*) have been found weighing as much as 260 kilograms, and may contain up to 200 litres of water.

During the brief rainy season, the desert erupts into life. Grasses spring up, annuals bloom and a host of insects emerge to feed on the pollen, nectar and fruits that abound. This is the season when many ungulates calve too. Although their calving cannot be triggered directly by the rains, since their gestation period lasts for several months, many species do synchronise their breeding cycles so as to give birth during or just before the anticipated arrival of the rains. Blue wildebeest, for example, calve early, and when the rains come and the Kalahari plains are clad in palatable young grasses, their herds already contain large nurseries of young.

This mass calving entails several advantages. Each year, predators account for a high percentage of calf mortalities and, during the breeding season, roving brown hyaenas circle the herds, looking out for vulnerable young. If large numbers of the offspring are born at once, at least some will survive to take advantage of the short season during which water and food are in plentiful supply.

Too soon, however, the brief rains are over. The pans slowly dry out and the Kalahari reverts to its thirsty barrenness. Now, the season of abundance over, the real test of survival is at hand.

During the dry season, animals and plants alike must contend with both the paucity of water and the extremes of temperature. On a daily basis, temperatures may fluctuate between 0 and 50 °C, necessitating further adaptations, particularly by the smaller Kalahari animals. The high daytime temperatures also increase the potential for water loss, resulting in a vicious cycle of hardship. The combination of these factors has resulted in the evolution of an astonishing array of adaptations to conditions in the Kalahari, both behavioural and physiological.

For plants, the problems are heightened in that they require sunlight to photosynthesise and so produce food, while this very exposure causes loss of water. Trees such as the mopane (*Colophospermum mopane*) have evolved mechanisms to

minimise such losses. During the heat of the day, the double leaflets of the mopane tree fold inwards towards each other, thereby reducing the surface area exposed to the sun.

The harsh conditions of the Kalahari mean that many plants are best able to succeed by passing the dry months in the form of dormant seeds. A profusion of seeds are produced towards the end of each rainy season, and most of these are dispersed by the dry winds of the Kalahari, deposited at last in the sand to await the next rains. The abundance of seeds, particularly of grasses, has resulted in the majority of birds in the Kalahari being seed-eaters. This diet has the disadvantage of containing very little water, and birds are forced either to diversify to other sources of food in addition to seeds, or to travel long distances in search of water.

BAOBABS – GIANT SUCCULENTS OF THE KALAHARI

Seen less often than the ubiquitous camelthorn of the Kalahari, the somewhat macabre baobab trees are nevertheless evocative of the smell and feel of the dry Kalahari. They are also trees of myth and legend. San legend holds that, in the beginning, the gods gave each animal a plant to cultivate. The hyaena was last in the queue, and when his turn came all that remained was the ugly baobab. In disgust, he planted it upside down. Other San legends relate how these trees have no seedling stage, but are sent down from heaven in their adult form. Being top-heavy, they land upside down and grow thereafter with their roots in the air.

It is easy to see from looking at these mammoth trees how these legends came about. The enormous trunk and slender yet simultaneously gnarled and twisted branches are more reminiscent of the root system of a tree than of its branches.

The wood of a baobab tree may hold up to 75 per cent water, and the immense tree thus constitutes an important water supply, particularly for elephants. During the dry season, elephants wreak tremendous harm on baobabs, ripping into their soft bark. Unlike other trees, the baobab is able to regenerate bark that has been thus gouged out.

Its fruit and seeds are eaten by many animals of the Kalahari. The white, pulpy flesh of the fruit contains an ascerbic substance, known as cream of tartar, which has exceptionally high concentrations of vitamin C. It is eagerly consumed by baboons and monkeys, from whence the tree derives its other name, the monkey-bread tree.

Baobabs are slow-growing, long-lived trees that may attain ages of several hundred years. The largest of succulents, when they finally die they are quickly reduced to a large fibrous heap.

The Burchell's sandgrouse (*Pterocles burchelli*) has taken the latter route. These birds, endemic to the Kalahari, are able to fly distances of up to 100 kilometres per day to the nearest waterhole, often converging in flocks of hundreds. The sandgrouse has evolved another important adaptation to life in the thirstlands. Although some pairs breed opportunistically immediately after rain, and often well into summer, in general they lay their eggs during the cooler months of the dry season, between April and August when food is more available. Moreover, during this time of year, the chicks, raised in a sandy scrape on the ground, are less likely to overheat. This advantage is offset, however, by the fact that by now water is in scant supply. Undaunted, the male sandgrouse has developed a unique method of transporting water to his offspring. His belly feathers comprise tightly coiled filaments that, when dry, are tightly spiralled around each other. When the feathers come into contact with water, the filaments uncoil and, through capillary action, trap water in the narrow spaces between them, acting much like blotting paper. Retaining water in this manner, the male then returns to his brood, and the chicks strip the feathers of the precious liquid. In true division of labour, only the male fulfills this role, the female's feathers probably being too out of condition from brooding the eggs to be able to hold water.

The animals of the Kalahari have also evolved a variety of methods of avoiding the heat. For many of them, these involve behavioural adaptations, and many animals are most active during the early evening or morning, disappearing into lairs, holes or nests in the heat of the day. Sociable weavers are one such species. These birds live in colonies, numbering several hundred birds. Their communal nests may be up to seven metres wide and comprise numerous small chambers. Within the nest, the birds are insulated by the thick layers of grass both from the high summer daytime temperatures and from the near-freezing temperatures of the winter nights. The nest structure is uniquely adapted to the aridity of the

Kalahari: under wetter conditions, the huge masses of grass would quickly deteriorate into rotting heaps of compost. Other birds also benefit from these sprawling weaver ghettos. The pygmy falcon (*Polihierax semitorquatus*), for example, is associated with sociable weaver nests, occupying empty chambers and preying on small insects or rodents in the vicinity. By contrast, other small animals take refuge from the heat in underground burrows or holes. Here, the deep sands both provide insulation from the heat and preserve moisture.

For larger animals such as the Kalahari ungulates – gemsbok and blue wildebeest, for example – it is less easy to take refuge in a hole or nest. These animals have adapted physiological mechanisms that enable them to survive the extreme temperatures of the thirstland. The large gemsbok (*Oryx gazella*), for example, absorbs heat slowly into its body throughout the day, and is able to withstand considerable increases in body temperature that, on reaching the brain, would normally result in death. Such tolerance is achieved by means of a cunning system that operates on the same principles as a car radiator. As hot blood approaches the brain, the arteries split into tiny capillaries, which pass closely by a similar network of tiny veins bringing cool blood back from the brain. Heat is exchanged between the arteries and the veins, and the cooled blood continues into the brain, passing through harmlessly, before circulating back into the rest of the body, via the branching veins, where it re-absorbs heat from incoming arteries. The overall body temperature of the animal remains high until evening, when the heat is lost by exposing the antelope's body to cool evening breezes blowing in over the gentle slopes of the sand ridges.

The Kalahari ungulates are faced with another problem: that of obtaining sufficient nutrients from largely indigestible material. During the dry season, food quality as a whole is low in the vegetation, which comprises primarily dry grasses and tough shrubs, consisting mainly of cellulose. In the larger ungulates, the problems of digesting this material have been partially overcome by the development of a multi-chambered stomach. In this organ, millions of resident micro-organisms slowly break down the tough cellulose into compounds that can be absorbed by the animal. The process, which involves fermentation of the plant material, is a slow one, and practical only for the bigger grazers such as eland and gemsbok that can ferment large volumes of food at a time.

For the smaller animals such as the dik-dik and the springbok, however, the emphasis is on food quality, rather than on quantity. These animals are highly particular about their food sources, carefully selecting only morsels that can be quickly digested. Springbok are thus mainly browsers, and eat grasses only during the rainy season, when the grass is fresh and high in protein. Even the gemsbok, primarily a grazer, supplements its diet with material such as gemsbok cucumbers and tsama melons, both of which have a high water content and contain additional proteins.

RIGHT: *Giant stalagmite at the entrance to Drotsky's Cave.*
BELOW: *Flowstone formations in caves beneath the Kalahari dolomite hills.*
BOTTOM LEFT: *Herds of springbok follow the patchy growth of grass across the Kalahari.*
BOTTOM RIGHT: *A snake leaves its tracks in the dry sands of the Kalahari.*

Some species of animals are unable to survive merely by switching diets between the seasons, and when water supplies have all but diminished and grazing material is low in quality, even the hardy springbok and resilient gemsbok cannot withstand the bleak aridity of the Kalahari indefinitely. At these times, the road to survival for many of the desert nomads is to set out for fresh pastures and new water holes. Thus begin the great migrations of grazer herds, followed by predators that will eke out their own survival by preying on the weak and dying, the young and the sick.

The great migrations

Early travellers, writing of the wonders of the arid interior of southern Africa, rarely fail to mention the awesome migrations of herds of grazing animals. Some accounts describe springbok herds numbering half a million animals at a time, moving like locusts across the land in their quest for fresh pastures and water supplies.

Less hardy than the springbok, and unable to survive without access to standing water, blue wildebeest (*Connochaetes taurinus*) migrate on a roughly annual basis, penetrating the Kalahari interior mainly during summer, when patchy rains trigger the growth of grazing material. As the long dry season begins to take its toll on grazing quality, the herds gather and move away.

Traditionally, blue wildebeest migrated north-west from the central Kalahari into the Okavango Delta. During the Kalahari dry season, the floodwaters of the Okavango River reach the floodplains of the lower delta, transforming them into a desert oasis. Grazing is plentiful in these grasslands, and the wildebeest were amongst many grazers that regularly found a dry season refuge there, to await the return of the rains to the Kalahari.

During the twentieth century, however, the wildlife spectacle of large-scale migrations came to an end as many of these migratory routes were impeded. In the 1960s and 1970s the Botswana government erected a series of veterinary cordon fences, designed to prevent the spread of foot-and-mouth disease between wild ungulates and the teeming herds of cattle. Little thought was given to the environmental consequences of these barriers, and the fences marched across the heart of the Kalahari, cutting off the great migratory routes and channelling the desperate herds into areas that offered inadequate water and grazing, leading to huge declines in wildebeest numbers.

Today, wildebeest and zebra, unable to penetrate the Okavango and the grazing regions around the Boteti River, are forced north towards Lake Xau. Here they compete with large herds of cattle for grazing and water. In desperation, the animals congregate in areas near artificial water sources. However, while water may be available here, grazing is not and the area surrounding Lake Xau has been trampled into a sandy wilderness. In this desolation, animals die in their thousands, their sun-bleached carcasses testifying to the ongoing devastation of the environment, and the deliberate destruction of a great natural phenomenon of southern Africa.

Kalahari caverns

While these desperate struggles for survival take place in the central and southern Kalahari, a range of low-lying hills in northern Botswana silently guards the secrets of the past. These are the Aha Hills, which rise abruptly out of the featureless landscape, their dolomite and limestone formations imparting a soft pink-

FAR LEFT: *Stalactites hang down from a cave roof beneath the Kalahari, in north-west Botswana.*
TOP: *The delicate "pearl" formation on the cave floor.*
ABOVE: *Rare lattice crystal formations on a cave wall.*
LEFT: *The velvety pods of the camelthorn tree are a valuable food resource for large ungulates.*
RIGHT: *Dry-season vegetation in the Aha Hills.*

ish hue to the horizon. Just south-east of these hills, the results of a long history of geological faulting and fracturing are evidenced in some of the most spectacular caves in southern Africa.

The most famous of these caves are the Gcwihaba Caverns, a San term meaning Lair of the Hyaena. The caves are also known as Drotsky's Caverns, after Martinus Drotsky, who was first shown the caves in 1932. The caves, located in a small outcrop, are set slightly above a fossil river bed, the Gcwihaba River. Over millennia of alternating wet and dry periods, this river was responsible for the gradual hollowing out and shaping of the caves. In fact, in the early stages of the caves' formation, the ancient river probably flowed some 30 metres above its present fossil bed. During a wetter period, it eroded the faulted dolomite, wearing away at the soft rock and forming the upper levels of today's impressive caverns. As the river cut sharply down through its bed, the water level dropped, and the lower levels of the caverns were formed.

It was during this wet period that the spectacular mineral formations within the caverns began. Rainfall was high and, as the water soaked through the ground above the caves, it dissolved salts out of the rocks. Mineral-laden water seeping slowly through the cave roofs evaporated into the caverns, leaving magnificent stalactites and flowstones that are still in evidence today. Time passed, and a dryer cycle began. The Gcwihaba River subsided, and finally dried up altogether, leaving the caves temporarily sealed by sand and straggling vegetation. Thereafter, a series of wet and dry periods followed, each wet period resulting in a gradual enlarging of the caves. The most recent of these wet periods occurred as recently as 2 000 years ago, when the last of the flowstones was deposited.

Today the Gcwihaba Caverns are inhabited by numerous bats, including Commerson's leaf-nosed bat (*Hipposideros commersoni*) and Dent's horseshoe bat (*Rhinolophus denti*). The cavern floors are littered with bat faeces and fragile skeletons, while the thick air is alive with their silent flitting between the stalactites.

Numerous other caves in this region have been similarly formed, and many others must lie as yet undiscovered beneath the rocky surfaces. Some of the caves yield rich fossil deposits, providing clues as to the kinds of animals that inhabited the region aeons ago. Caves are grand accumulators of fossils, since leopards, hyaenas and other predators bring their prey into such places to feed. Skeletons and other fragments of long-dead animals collect in the caves, fossilised within their silent confines.

ABOVE: *Arid savanna vegetation of the Kalahari.*
RIGHT: *Mokolwane palms (Hyphaene petersiana) at Makgadikgadi Pans.*
FAR RIGHT: *Bushman paintings in the Tsodilo Hills show an abundance of animal species, many of which are now long absent from the Kalahari.*

Land of legend

South of the Aha Hills, the flat expanses of the Kalahari are once again broken by a number of rocky outcrops or inselbergs rising abruptly from the grey-brown veld, like islands in a sea of aridity. These are the Tsodilo Hills, a collection of hills comprising four distinct formations, three of which are known as the Male, the Female and the Child. The fourth hill is unnamed, and legend holds that this hill is the first wife of the Male, shunned and cast away when he took his second wife, the Female.

The hills hold great spiritual significance for the local people, both San and Hambukushu, the latter believing that their early ancestors were delivered to earth along with their goats and cattle, by their god, Nyambe, who deposited them on the Female. For the San, the hills are the birthplace of the gods, who now live and rule from compartments within the Female.

Unlike the Aha Hills, the Tsodilo Hills, and the Female in particular, are rich in rock paintings. It is believed that these paintings, some dating back to between AD 800 and 1300, others from a more recent age, were done by the San. The San themselves believe that the paintings were the work of their god Gaoxa. These paintings show great skill and are of particular interest in their depiction of scenes and animals, some of which have now been lost forever. One painting shows a creature resembling a whale. Whether this was the product of an ancestral traveller who actually crossed the vast distance to the sea, or merely an aberration of a large fish once resident in the former superlake, remains debatable.

Today like most arid areas of the world, the Kalahari is fortunate in that large areas have been declared reserves, albeit only because these areas are perceived to be of little value to humans. Ironically, however, while the lack of water and barren landscape have played a vital role in protecting this unique landscape from the ravages of man, it sounds, at the same time, as a knell of doom for the oasis of the Kalahari, the Okavango wetland, where the lush waterways of the delta are all the more alluring to developers, set against the arid backdrop of the thirstlands.

BELOW: Pachydactylus, *a gecko found on the gypsum of the pans.*
OVERLEAF: *A lesser flamingo stretches in an "inverted wing salute" – a formalised and ritualistic display performed prior to breeding.*

GREAT TREKS OF THE FLAMINGOS

Etosha and Makgadikgadi are probably the only areas in southern Africa where flamingos breed on a large scale. Even here they breed erratically, the timing of breeding depending on the availability of large areas of shallow water in the pans. When conditions appear favourable, they come into breeding plumage, with the red feathers of greater flamingos (*Phoenicopterus ruber*) developing into a deeper hue, while lesser flamingos (*P. minor*) become suffused with pink throughout.

Their courtship routines are colourful displays of stately grandeur, involving complex routines performed en masse, each aimed at displaying a maximum amount of black and red feathers. Courtship is only followed by mating if environmental conditions remain favourable. Pairs then form and nest building begins. Different groups of birds within the colony will mate at different times, resulting in a continuum of stages in egg-brooding and age class of young. As a general rule, those flamingos that hatch first will be most likely to survive, while late-hatchers risk the pans drying out before they are able to fly.

Both sexes contribute towards nest-building, and the nests comprise raised mounds of salty clay surrounded by shallow moats, scooped out by beak. In the raised nests, temperatures are a few degrees lower than on the surrounding mud flats, an attribute probably vital to the survival of the young flamingos. Flamingo chicks grow quickly, and when they are one week old, they huddle in large groups on the mud flats while their parents are away feeding. Young adults known as "nursemaids" tend the nurseries, which often number thousands of chicks. Incredibly, chicks and their parents are able to recognise each other's calls, and parents feed only their own young.

The erratic breeding behaviour of flamingos is explained in terms of the range of potentially fatal disasters that may beset their chicks: it is only worth breeding when risks of mortality are lowest. The most common causes of death to young flamingos are flooding of the nests by rising water levels, or, alternatively, premature drying out of the pans. Young flamingos are able to fly at the age of 10 or 11 weeks. Until this time, however, they are utterly dependent on the availability of water close at hand, and on the food provided by their parents. As the pans dry up, chicks that are as yet unable to fly are faced with only two options: remain and die, or walk to the nearest water. They set off across the scorching clay, walking in long straggling columns of desperate birds, probably guided by nursemaids flying overhead.

Some of the young will survive, reaching sources of water that have not yet been lost to the searing heat or sucked into the thirsty clays. They are fed along the way by their parents, who commute desperately between distant water sources and their offspring. However, the routes of these tragic crusades are marked with the tiny, fragile skeletons of chicks that succumbed to the wastelands. The drying clays form death traps for the weakening birds, with salty encrustations forming around their legs and weighing them down.

CHAPTER 4

In the heart of the Kalahari, the mighty Okavango River
spills out across the flat sands, its delta forming an intricate
network of clear waters and reed-lined channels: a mosaic of blues
and greens set incongruously against the dry monotony of the sur-
rounding thirstland. One of the world's few inland deltas, the
Okavango must be one of Africa's most enchanted places.

Huge flocks of red-billed queleas roost in the delta.

Lechwe jumping through the shallow waters of the swamp.

Water lily (Nymphaea spp.).

THE *Okavango Delta*

THIRSTLAND OASIS

LEFT: *Aerial view of lagoons in the perennial swamp: large areas of open water separated by reedbeds, and connected by narrow channels, kept open by the passage of hippo.*
RIGHT: *Red-billed quelea (Quelea quelea).*

I n this desert oasis a wetland wilderness of unrivalled beauty provides both habitat and dry-season refuge for a multitude of animals and plants, some inhabiting the delta permanently, others coming and going with the changing rhythms of the Kalahari.

Geological evidence suggests that the Okavango Delta is the remnant of what was once a vast lake that spread across the Kalahari, incorporating the Makgadikgadi Pans. The exact history of the Okavango River and its course is, however, open to debate. Some proponents hold that it once joined the Chobe and upper Zambezi Rivers, forming a massive waterway that flowed across the Kalahari and entered the upper Limpopo River. Subsequently, subterranean movements resulted in the ponding-back of this section of the Limpopo, to create an inland sea. In time, this superlake itself fell victim to tectonic forces as southerly extensions of the East African Rift Valley deflected the upper Zambezi and Chobe Rivers eastward to join the middle Zambezi, leaving the Okavango trapped in the Rift Valley's most southerly trough. As climates changed, the river was reduced to a fraction of its past extent and today, 95 per cent of its volume is lost to evaporation in the searing heat of the Kalahari.

Today the Okavango River rises on the Benguela Plateau, in the distant heights of the Angola highlands. Here, known as the Cubango River, it flows in a wide, green-fringed channel as far as the northern border of Namibia, where it crosses the Caprivi panhandle and in so doing is confined within a flat valley some 10 to 15 kilometres wide. In this region, the river flows swiftly along a

single, steep-banked channel, divided on the surface by floating papyrus rafts that form an ever-changing maze.

The sandy banks are lined with graceful wild date palms (*Phoenix reclinata*), the dominant tree on the outer fringes of islands, and thickets of gomoti or water fig (*Ficus verruculosa*) trees, while water lilies (*Nymphaea* spp.) spread delicately across the shallow backwaters and lagoons.

In the silence of the waterways, the call of the fish eagle (*Haliaeetus vocifer*) sounds uncannily, and an astonishing diversity of other birds feed on the rich harvest of aquatic life. This is also the home of Pel's fishing owl (*Scotopelia peli*), whose deep hoots and occasional male-female duets reverberate across the night-time waters. This bird fishes at night, and the mechanism that allows its skillful location of fish in the darkness remains a mystery.

The permanent swamps

Some 95 kilometres downstream, the river passes out of the panhandle and onto the flat expanse of the Kalahari sands. With no fault lines to restrict its course, it widens out into a vast delta, dividing repeatedly to form an intricate network of shallow, slow-flowing channels lined with dense clusters of bulrushes (*Typha capensis*) and beds of reeds.

The water in these reaches is clear, and one can see the silver glint of fish moving through the weeds and lily stems beneath. The clarity of the water here is due to the combination of flat terrain and the abundance of wetland vegetation that characterises this part of the delta. The slow meander of the river across an almost flat surface causes it to drop the silt and debris carried down from the highlands, while the vegetation acts as a purifying filter, absorbing nutrients from the water and preventing subsequent growth of algae that would reduce water clarity. Papyrus (*Cyperus papyrus*) is a particularly effective filter, being able to absorb nutrients even when its concentrations are low. As old papyrus stalks die off, these nutrients are reabsorbed into the main plant, leaving the old stalk dry and papery. The delta water itself remains generally low in nutrients, and thus not prone to excessive blooms of green algal growths.

In this region of the delta, the perennial swamp comprises a labyrinth of reed and papyrus-lined channels, permanently inundated with water. The dense vegetation is a paradise for birds, and the harsh boom of the dwarf bittern (*Ixobrychus sturmii*), resonating from the wetland thickets at dusk and in the stillness of early morning, is symbolic of these reaches. A wide variety of birds inhabit the inner swamp, and move easily between the cover of the reedbeds and the rich feeding grounds in the shallow backwaters, flying overhead or navigating along the narrow water channels.

Animals lacking these aerial powers find the swamp more restrictive, however, and few large mammals are able to penetrate into its heart. A strong swimmer, the shy sitatunga (*Tragelaphus spekei*) is the only large mammal that inhabits the permanent swamp zone exclusively. Its elongated hooves, measuring up to 18 centimetres long, are adapted to running through the thick mud and matted vegetation, splaying out to spread its weight across a wider surface area, while its raised hindquarters allow it to lope quietly through the thick reeds. In these dense areas its predators are few, and the most serious threat to the sitatunga, other than the ubiquitous influence of man, is crocodiles, which lurk in the shaded waterways. If alarmed, sitatunga take flight, or submerge themselves beneath the water with just their nostrils showing.

Sitatunga calves are born on platforms of flattened reeds in the heart of the swamp. Here the calves remain, concealed behind dense clumps of reeds, until they are strong enough to cope with the rigours of the inner swamp. Difficult as the terrain is, however, food in the swamp is plentiful for this reclusive antelope, which is the only mammal to feed predominantly on papyrus, using its teeth to half snap the tall stalks so that the soft flower heads droop limply down and are easily browsed.

FAR LEFT: *The cry of the African fish eagle epitomises this wetland wilderness.*
LEFT: *Thick beds of papyrus form effective filters, contributing to the astounding clarity of the swamp water.*
BELOW: *Rapid evaporation of water results in the formation of hyper-saline pans.*
OPPOSITE: *Prolonged immersion of tree roots resulting from flooding due to hippo activities, led to the formation of places such as Dead Tree Island.*

Other mammals found in the waterways of the permanent swamp are otters, both Cape clawless (*Aonyx capensis*) and the spotted-necked (*Lutra maculicollis*) species. Hippo (*Hippopotamus amphibius*) are also abundant here and play a vital role in maintaining the open water channels, allowing water to flush through the system and percolate slowly south. They have a peculiar advantage over other mammals when it comes to navigating through the swamp. With large males weighing up to 1,5 tonnes, these rotund animals have little difficulty in ploughing their own paths through the swamp channels as they move between grazing grounds on the river banks and their daytime wallows in the cool waters. Their ponderous passage between areas of low-lying ground results at times in new areas being opened up to the floodwaters, as their paths form connecting passages of lower ground.

Dead Tree Island is one such area where hippo have altered the flooding pattern. Wooded meadows, once cut off from the river channel by vegetation and raised banks, are now inundated, thanks to the hippo that broke through, undaunted by the vegetation, and brought with them first trickles and then channels of water. Today, the tall trees of the woodland stand white and dead, their trunks extending naked from the still pools of water.

RIGHT: *Termite mounds add heterogeneity to the flat delta surface and may eventually result in the formation of new islands.*
BELOW: *Deep open-water channels provide yet another habitat type within the delta.*

ABOVE: *The poor waterproofing of the darter's feathers are an adaptation to allow it to dive after prey, which it spears with its sharp beak. As a trade-off, the bird must dry its wings in the air on emerging from the water.*
ABOVE RIGHT: *At night, the swamp resounds to the calls of amphibians such as this,* Bufo gutturalis.

In the waters beneath

Beneath the surface of the swamp, the biological pulse is as strong as it is above. The filtering actions of the papyrus and reedbeds in the panhandle upstream result in the water of the permanent swamp being generally low in nutrients, and some organisms have developed extraordinary mechanisms to survive in these conditions. The strange bladderwort plant (*Utricularia* sp.), for example, has neither roots nor leaves. Instead it comprises hundreds of tiny bladders, which it uses as traps to snare mosquito and other insect larvae abundant in the quiet waters of the delta. When a larva touches a bladder, the bladder pouch expels water from one side, thereby creating a suction effect on the other. This serves to draw the unfortunate insect inside. In the bladder, it is digested by micro-organisms and the precious nutrients contained in its body tissue are utilised by the plant for growth.

In the waterways, floating mats of aquatic vegetation create their own particular environments. Beneath them, the water is cold and dark. With little light passing through to allow plant growth, the water is consequently often low in oxygen. Nevertheless, it still provides a habitat for many animals. Among these are the predatory diving beetles (members of the family Dytiscidae), which like miniature scuba divers carry their own supply of air with them. When they surface, they trap air bubbles between their abdomens and their hard elytras. The bubbles are slowly used up as they dive down again, searching for prey.

The darkness beneath the floating mats also provides a refuge for small fish from predators such as tigerfish (*Hydrocynus vittatus*) that lurk in the main channels of the delta. Others, such as squeaker fish (*Synodontis nygromaculatus*) avoid predation by feeding at night. Sensory barbels on the sides of squeakers' heads enable them to detect insect larvae. By day, they hide beneath logs and vegetation mats, while sharp spines on their dorsal and pectoral fins deter predators. When a squeaker is consumed, their spines lock into a rigid position in the luckless predator's gullet, often resulting in death. Of course, some determined feeders have circumvented this problem. The reed cormorant (*Phalacrocorax africanus*) searches for squeakers by diving, emerging with the fish grasped firmly in its beak. With great dexterity, the bird manoeuvres its catch into position on a log or on the river bank, before plunging its lower beak through the back of the squeaker's head, and into its gills. Killed instantly this way, the squeaker has no time to lock its spines in position and the cormorant completes its meal in comfort.

Islands of the south

As the delta extends southwards, it widens and begins to dry out. This is one of the unique features of the Okavango: unlike most deltas, it is doomed by a quirk of tectonics and geological patterns never to reach the sea, but to dissipate slowly in the thirstlands. Its only outlet is the Thamalakane River, which is diverted by the fault of the same name, and joins another rivulet, thus forming the Boteti River. In a good year, this river flows through Lake Xau and extends as far as the Makgadikgadi Pans, bringing to life the dry, salt-encrusted sands. At the same time, this outlet, albeit infrequent, prevents the Okavango Delta from slowly salting up. Salts brought into the system by the Okavango River are thus removed. Only in some areas, such as on the perimeters of the islands in the south – raised spits of Kalahari sand protruding into the wetland – is evaporation so fast that white powdery crystals of salt are left in sun-baked rings around the shoreline.

These islands, the edges of which lie less than one metre above the water level, are characterised by these white efflorescent crystals, known locally as *ntsongo*. The crystal rings are formed when groundwater, fed by the carbonate-rich surface waters of the delta, is drawn up around the edges of the island by a process known as capillary action. As the water evaporates on the island surface, tiny crystals form. Calcite, one of the intermediate products of this crystallisation, is formed between the sand grains, and used by termites in the construction of their mounds.

In the south, the large, white-ringed islands are a characteristic feature of the landscape, and include Chief's Island. These islands stand out in stark contrast to the verdant waterways surrounding them. Most comprise thick stands of mopane woodland, consisting primarily of large mopane trees (*Colophospermum mopane*), interspersed with lower-growing species such as the broad-leaved shepherd's tree (*Boscia mossambicensis*). Mopane trees provide an important food source for

SOCIAL LIFE AND SAUSAGE TREES

As the floodwaters subside, and the plains and *melapo* sprout luxuriant grasses, the sausage tree (*Kigelia africana*) becomes a centre of attraction. During the warm, still nights the rich maroon flowers give off a pungent odour, which attracts small bats. These tiny creatures, some carrying young suspended precariously from their backs, are responsible for much of the fertilisation of these exotic flowers, which give rise eventually to the spectacular sausage-shaped fruit from which the tree derives its name.

The bats are not the only animals attracted to the rich harvest of flowers. By day, a multitude of birds and vervet monkeys are to be found, daintily sipping nectar from the trumpet-shaped flowers, while the less fastidious baboons wrench whole flowers from their stalks, munching them contentedly. In the dappled shade below the tree, impala graze distractedly, waiting for the real prize of the site: flowers dropped by the gorging baboons.

A few months later, the flowers that survived the eager throngs of browsers fall heavily to the ground as fruits. With some fruits weighing up to 10 kilograms, they represent no small find, and are consumed by those animals strong enough to break through their tough outer covering: elephant, hippo, baboon and occasionally even the lithesome giraffe. Traditionally, the fruits are hung in African huts to provide protection from whirlwinds.

animals of the delta. Their leaves have a high protein content, and are eagerly sought out by browsers. For many animals, however, the availability of free-standing water is more important than the presence of food. The grey clay soil underlying much of the mopane woodland retains water, allowing the shallow inland pans to hold both rainwater and groundwater for some time into the dry season. These watering spots provide a temporary refuge for many animals during the early months of the dry season.

The pulse of the delta

While the longitudinal changes in habitat, channel form and vegetation between the start of the narrow panhandle and the southern extremity of the Okavango Delta are intriguing, it is in the seasonal pulse of water through the channels that the intricate patterns and delicately interrelated functions of the wetland are revealed. Surprisingly, it is not the local rains falling in the delta itself between November and March that account for these pulses of water through the system. Instead, the delta depends for its life-force on events occurring upstream, in the highlands of Angola.

Rain falling in the upper catchment in summer (November to March) swells the headwaters of the river. These floods move downstream, held back by the vegetation and the flatness of the land. The panhandle itself receives floodwaters quite soon after the rainy season (February or March) but the southern regions of the delta may wait until June for the long fingers of water to reach them.

TOP: *Rain clouds mass behind the delta. These rains will bring new growth to the seasonal grasslands, but it is the rain that falls in Angola that will flood the delta months later.*
ABOVE: *Out of the main current, delicate water plants flourish.*
FAR LEFT: *A herd of alert red lechwe grazes in the flooded meadows: crocodiles are the biggest threat in these shallows.*
LEFT: *Herds of elephant converge to drink and wallow in the waters of the delta.*

In the Okavango Delta itself, the arrival of the floods is preceded by weeks of anticipation, the entire system poised to take advantage of the abundance that inevitably follows. This season coincides with the Kalahari dry season, rendering the season of plenty still more extravagant in contrast to the barren sands of the surrounding land.

The first sign of the approaching floods is given by the upstream migration of barbel (*Clarias* spp.), the whiskered catfish of the swamps. Large shoals begin to move northwards, congregating in the main channels of the panhandle. Here, smaller fish are plentiful, driven into the mainstream by the receding waters, and the barbel exploit them to the full. Working in packs, they flush the fish out from the shelter of the reedbeds, their bodies thrashing against the protective vegetation. The fish are consumed in a churning frenzy that attracts both predatory birds and local fishermen. When the first pulses of floodwater surge slowly into the delta, however, the barbel move into their spawning grounds in the freshly submerged grasses of the floodplain.

As the floodwaters move slowly downstream, the landscape changes dramatically. The channels fill and spill over into shallow meadows or *melapo*. In these sheltered backwaters, water lilies quickly grow up, their long stems providing a refuge for small fish, insect larvae and amphibians. Here the waters are too shallow for large predatory fish such as the tigerfish (*Hydrocynus vittatus*), which are largely restricted to the main channels. Procreation is the name of the game, and

ABOVE LEFT: *Crocodile* (Crocodylus niloticus) *basking on a sandbank.*
FAR LEFT: *Sunlight glistens on a large spider web – deathly but beautiful trap of the delta.*
LEFT: *A yellow-billed stork uses its feet to herd fish towards its beak.*
ABOVE: *Carmine bee-eater nests in a river bank.*

at night the warm air throbs to a cacophony of sounds, as shrill crickets vie with the rhythmic beat of courting frogs. Male reed frogs (*Hyperolius* spp.) solicit females by calling raucously from their slender reed territories.

The warm sheltered waters of the flooded *melapo* are also utilised as breeding grounds for several other species of fish. However, the standing water means that oxygen is often in low supply. African pike (*Hepsetus odoe*) overcome this problem by laying their eggs in foam nests. These float near the surface where oxygen supplies are better. Extra skin flaps on the sides of their mouths are used to create the bubbles of foam, and the parents maintain the frothy nests for some time even after the young have hatched.

Other fish have adapted their behaviour to survive the low oxygen conditions in the *melapo*. Striped top-minnows (for example *Aplocheilichthys katangae*) inhabit the upper surfaces of the water, which are better oxygenated. This strategy has its price, however, as the little fish are highly vulnerable to predators. One such predator is the remarkable fishing spider (an example being *Thalassius leonensis*).

The small hooks on the rear legs of the spider anchor it to floating vegetation, while its body floats motionless on the water surface. When the top-minnow comes within range, the spider sinks its powerful jaws into the minnow's flesh, emitting a deadly toxin as it does so. As well as killing the fish, the toxin also dissolves its body tissue, allowing the spider to suck it up as fluid.

The fish of the *melapo* are not only vulnerable to spiders. The shallow waters make them an easy target for a multitude of water birds, many of which have adapted their life-cycles to take full advantage of the season of plenty. Storks, egrets and herons hunt the waters with a determined eye, the yellow-billed stork (*Mycteria ibis*) using its long legs to herd fish towards its beak. Other water birds such as jacanas are also highly adapted to life in the shallow pans. Their elongated toes spread their weight over a wide area, enabling them to move nimbly across the lily pads without sinking. Both species of jacana occurring in the Okavango – the African and the lesser jacana – nest in floating masses of aquatic vegetation, their eggs glossy to mimic the sheen of water amongst the reeds.

In nesting and parental care, the African jacana (*Actophilornis africanus*) displays a singular role reversal, with the male bird both incubating the eggs and subsequently caring for the chicks. The species has evolved a peculiar adaptation to parental care by way of a bow-shaped radius, or inner "wrist-bone". The shape of this limb enables the brooding male to tuck his wing in beneath him, holding the eggs on the wing and so elevating them above the damp nest. When the eggs hatch, the chicks are highly mobile and are able to feed themselves within a few hours. They remain close to their parent, however, and when danger threatens the chicks are scooped up and carried to safety, clutched against the bow of his wing.

Other waterfowl show less concern over the fate of their young, as they jostle to exploit the abundant food supplies of the flooded delta. During the breeding season, male maccoa ducks *(Oxyura maccoa)* assume a handsome chestnut plumage and bright blue bill, which they display with the vanity of a dandy, treating females to displays of paddling and vigorous trumpeting. The males are promiscuous and mate with several females, the latter showing a similar disinclination for responsibility, and frequently depositing their eggs into the nests of other more maternal birds.

OPPOSITE TOP AND BOTTOM: *Voracious seed-eaters, red-billed queleas need a constant supply of water and come in their thousands to drink and roost in the delta. When the flock flies away in the morning, tiny quelea corpses remain, transfixed on acacia thorns by the multitude of birds around them during the previous night.*
ABOVE LEFT: *Sunset in the delta.*
ABOVE: *Lions are abundant in the Okavango where their prey gathers in high concentrations.*
LEFT: *Children play in the river, celebrating the seasonal return of water to the delta.*

As the cool, dry months of the Kalahari winter pass, the floods of the Okavango subside and retreat back into the reed-lined channels of the perennial swamps. With the dryness, however, a new land of plenty is unleashed. The floodplains are enriched with detritus accumulated whilst submerged. Now warm, damp and above the waterline, grasses spring up, and soon the once lily-bedecked *melapo* sport a thick turf of grass. While the surrounding Kalahari slowly parches, turning grey-brown in the months that must elapse before the rains, the Okavango abounds in food. For many grazers this, more than the flood season, is the time of revival.

Red lechwe antelope (*Kobus leche*) move with the rise and fall of the waters, keeping to the edge of the grasslands where they are able to graze fresh grass shoots growing up through the receding water, the birth of their calves timed to coincide with this period of new growth on the floodplains. Like the sitatunga, the lechwe has elongated hooves, adapted to support it over swampy terrain. Propelled by its powerful hindquarters, it is able to run faster through the shallow waters than across dry land.

Creatures that shape the land

As the floodplains slowly dry out, terrestrial processes that shape the delta further south can be observed. While the role of hippo is vital in maintaining the open waterways of the swamp, it is a tiny termite that is often responsible for the creation of small islands. Fungus termites (*Macrotermes mossambicus*) build large mounds on the floodplains and in the *melapo*, using saliva and calcite to cement

the tiny grains of sand together. The mounds grow quickly, laboured on by teams of worker ants. The termites are photophobic, and build covered runs between the mound and their source of food (usually dead wood). This food has a high lignin and cellulose content, and is only partially digested by the workers. Back in the mound, it is expelled as faeces and left, where it is colonised by fungus.

The fungus and the termites share a remarkable symbiotic relationship. The fungi convert the cellulose and lignin to proteins, which are fed by the workers to young termites and to the breeding pair. Meanwhile, the mound continues to increase in size, growing up from an ever-widening base. If two or more termite mounds are built in close proximity, their bases will eventually join, forming a ridge of higher ground. When this happens in the narrow entrances to the *melapo*, the mounds block the seasonal flow of floodwater into the meadows. In time, grasses give way to woody vegetation and trees and shrubs grow up.

The cycle is self-perpetuating, as large ant mounds trap silt and debris around them, slowly growing into small hills, which form islands during the flood season. These hills also have a role to play, acting as vantage points for antelope such as lechwe. Abandoned mounds are used as nests or shelters for a range of other animals, including monitor lizards, which use them to incubate their eggs.

The termites themselves continue with their frenetic cycle of building, feeding and reproduction. Life in the mound is geared towards one central point in the annual cycle: the coming of the rains, when winged castes of fertile termites (called alates) leave the nest in droves and disperse into other areas of the delta. Those alates that survive the feeding frenzy of swooping birds form breeding pairs on the ground, shedding their wings and beginning a new cycle of breeding and mound construction.

The coming of the rains

The build-up to the rains seems interminable. A thick grey heat settles over the delta and promising clouds build up daily, only to fragment and disappear in smoky wisps. At last, however, the clouds break. Lightning forks the sky, and the first large, warm drops of rain bounce off the dusty ground.

The rains mark the start of a new phase of life in the delta. With the first storm, winged termites struggle from opened holes in their natal mounds, pause, then launch themselves off the ground in jerky flight. Their flight is perhaps symbolic, for with the rains begins an exodus from the delta. Rains fall in the Kalahari itself at this time, and the herds of antelope and their retinue of predators for whom the delta is but a dry season refuge, return to the Kalahari plains for the

PAINTED DOGS OF THE OKAVANGO

A light breeze picks up in the late afternoon and sets up a dry rustling in the mopane woodland. In the dusty grass, a large, rounded ear twitches expectantly, followed by a nose, and then the patchy black, white and yellow body of an African wild dog emerges, stretching and sniffing the air. This is a signal to the rest of the pack, rousing them from their siestas for the evening's work. Soon the whole pack, numbering some 10 or 11 dogs, are running around excitedly, sniffing each other and occasionally yipping. A few minutes later they set off through the scrub, one animal taking the lead while the others follow at a gentle trot. The young pups of this year's litter are left behind, watched over by a yearling.

The African wild dog (*Lycaon pictus*) is the largest wild canid in Africa and has inhabited Africa for as long as, if not longer than man has. Living in packs that may number as many as 40 animals at times, these dogs, also known as "painted dogs" because of their distinctive markings, have a well-developed social structure. Each pack is led by a dominant male and female that mate and remain bonded until one of them dies. This pair is responsible for producing litters of pups each year, while the rest of the pack, usually comprising sub-ordinate siblings and offspring of the dominant pair, help with rearing the young and hunting for food.

Wild dogs hunt medium-sized antelope, and in the Okavango Delta, lechwe and impala are important prey. Each pack of dogs has its own territory, covering 400 to 450 square kilometres in areas such as the delta where food is relatively abundant. Dogs mark the territory by urinating along its perimeter, the smell informing other groups of wild dogs that the territory is occupied. The pack roams at will through this territory, only returning to a particular area when there are pups that require feeding in an underground den.

Wild dogs are extremely efficient hunters, working in groups to bring down large animals that one dog alone would probably be unable to capture. Antelope are high-risk prey items because of their size and strength relative to those of the wild dog and even a wounded antelope is capable of inflicting severe injury or even death. It is thus critical to the success of the pack that the kill be accomplished as efficiently as the hunt. The fallen antelope is therefore disembowelled with expert speed, the sharp teeth of the dogs cutting into the soft belly of the animal, and then snipping upwards to remove the liver, heart and lungs. Thus disembowelled, the prey is set upon by the dogs. They eat quickly, to reduce the chances of kills being lost to other carnivores, and if there are young pups in the pack, each dog returns to the den and feeds the eager waiting pups by regurgitating some of the fresh meat.

brief season of fertility. Other animals migrate to the interiors of the larger islands. Buffalo, only present near the waterways during the dry season, cross over to these islands in large herds, and move inland to the central areas of mopane woodland and grasslands.

The rain-induced exodus from the floodplain just as the grasses begin to sprout appears paradoxical at first. However, in spite of their abundance, the floodplain grasses are coarse and have a lower nutrient content than the sweet but sparser grass of the island interiors. As long as sufficient water remains in the small clay water pans of the island interiors, these grazers may remain.

While the delta rains bring temporary water to the inland pans and generate fresh growths of grass, they have no influence on the shrinking water level of the swamp. The water recedes to a few main channels, and wide sand banks are exposed along the river banks. Some animals have been waiting for just this event. As evening falls in the panhandle, African skimmers (*Rynchops flavirostris*) begin their long slow flights over the shimmering waters, their eyes adapted to the poor light. Unlike many other waterfowl they delay breeding until the water is low enough for extensive stretches of sand bank to be available, where they lay their eggs in shallow scoops.

The sand banks are also used by a more ominous member of the Okavango community. As the floodwaters subside, female crocodiles (*Crocodylus niloticus*) lumber slowly up the river bank, and lay between 20 and 90 eggs in a nest. The eggs are covered with sand and incubated for about three months. Temperature differentials play an important role in determining the sexes of the offspring, with male crocodiles emerging from the warmer surface eggs and females from below. During incubation, the female crocodile remains near the nest. When the eggs are ready to hatch, the baby crocodiles emit a squeak, which alerts her to their presence. She scrapes away the sand from the nest, and assists the babies to the water.

Both crocodiles and skimmers must rear their young before the floods of the new season reach the swamps from Angola and cover the sand banks. Meanwhile in the delta, the fresh green growth of grass brought on by the rains has browned and the inland pans are beginning to disappear. Once again, the air of expectation slowly mounts. The rains that will once more swell the banks of the river and fill the *melapo* have already fallen in their distant headwaters and are slowly making their way down towards the vast wetland. In the drying Kalahari, the thirsty herds prepare once more for their long journey across the plains to the abundance of the Okavango Delta.

The tectonic forces that played such an important role in the creation
of the desolate wilderness of the Kalahari and its wetland oasis, the
Okavango Delta, were also responsible for the formation of a differ-
ent series of systems nearly 2 000 kilometres away — the great lakes
of the East African Rift Valley, of which Lake Malawi remains one
of the most undisturbed and breathtakingly beautiful.

Cichlids shoal in the deep waters of the lake.

Exploding pods of the Bauhinia *tree.*

Dry summer vegetation on one of the islands.

LAKE Malawi AND THE Shire Valley

EDENS OF THE RIFT VALLEY

LEFT: *A large catch of usipa, a sardine-like fish found in Lake Malawi.*
RIGHT: *A local man carves a dugout canoe from hardwood.*

Malawi, land of the lake. The name sums up the importance, at least to this tiny country, of the vast water body that occupies nearly one-fifth of Malawi's entire surface area, and supplies home, food, water and a lucrative tourist industry to a people with a burgeoning population and scant resources. Lake Malawi is in fact the third largest lake in Africa and the most southerly of a series of seven lakes, each formed within a section of the 3 000 kilometre long series of rift valleys that extend like a ragged scar from North Africa down as far as Zambia.

The processes that both gave rise to this lake and played a role in the formation of the Kalahari Edens described in earlier chapters began some 20 million years ago when, pulled by tensions deep within the earth, this section of Africa slowly tore apart, creating a deep trench between ranges of uplifted mountains. Over time, water accumulated in the steep-sided valleys, forming natural lakes that eventually found their own outlets and developed drainage routes to the sea. Lake Malawi itself is estimated at only about three million years old, but with a length of 580 kilometres and a width of up to 85 kilometres in parts, it is the eleventh largest lake in the world.

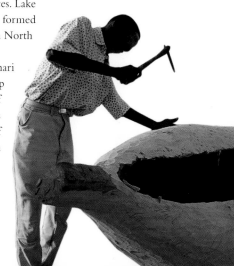

There is enough cold fact here to satisfy any collector of trivial information. To concentrate on these, however, is to ignore the essence of Lake Malawi and its associated waterways, and to reduce its hazy warmth and blue clarity to mere figures in a text book. For while the scale of the lake is imposing, stretching horizonless out from the shores and more like a sea than a conventional lake, it is in its more intimate detail that its true interest lies, at least to the naturalist. Lake Malawi and the land and rivers abutting and intimately linked to it contain a diversity of habitat, flora and fauna that cannot be guessed at from the aerial photographs displaying its magnitude.

In the north, the sides of the Rift Valley plunge for the most part steeply down into the clear waters of the lake, the escarpment of the imposing Nyika Plateau dropping down to the water's edge. At this level, sheer cliffs and occasional sandy coves mark the shore, while above the *Brachystegia* woodland common to many of the Malawi slopes rises up towards the plateau itself, the new leaves glowing in warm oranges and reds during the spring months, then brightening to summer greens, before finally dropping off.

Further south along the lake, the enclosing sides of the escarpment fall back, and the lake is bounded by a wide fringe of sandy shore, dotted with palm trees and occasional banana plants. Coupled with the thick heat and clear blue water, the impression is overwhelmingly tropical – almost clichéd in its conformity to the tropical-island stereotype. Further away from the lake, where cultivation has not created its own vegetation types, the beaches give way to forests of stately

RIGHT: *The blue waters of Lake Malawi, seen from Momba Island.*
BELOW: *Dawn breaks over Lake Malawi from Otter Point, near Cape Maclear.*

BELOW LEFT: Impatiens *are just one of the delicate flowers that thrive on the cool heights and damp hollows of Nyika Plateau.*
BELOW: *Orchids provide delicate splashes of colour on Nyika Plateau. Shown here are species of* Eulophia *(centre) and the rare* Disa erubescens *(right).*

baobabs and then to drier grasslands or woodlands. Along the shore, patches of reedy swampland occur in sheltered areas, providing wetlands where diverse arrays of animals congregate.

In the far south, the lake has its only outlet, the Shire River, which meanders slowly south through shallow Lake Malombe and across a broad floodplain towards its confluence with the Zambezi River some 480 kilometres downstream. The languid river gains momentum only briefly during its course, between Malope and the Kapichira Falls, where for some 80 kilometres potholes, rapids, waterfalls and the narrow Mpatamanga Gorge send the water thundering through rocky channels, hemmed in by the spray-saturated sides of the steep escarpment.

The inlets and the high places

While Lake Malawi has only one outlet, it is fed by many small streams, as well as by 14 larger rivers. One of these, the North Rukuru River, rises high on the Nyika Plateau in the north west of Malawi and within the largest conservation area in the country, the Nyika National Park. On the heights of the plateau, the tropical heat of the lowland valleys is a memory of the past. Here, the air is bracing and, during the cool dry season in the middle of the year, sprinklings of ground frost are common. Indeed, in some respects the landscape is disconcertingly European, with rolling grasslands extending in unlikely swathes of green across the plateau slopes.

Rainfall is high in this region and wetlands, small seeps and trickling waterfalls are common. In the sheltered folds of the hills, pockets of montane forest persist and both within these forests and in the surrounding grassveld, some of the most sought after prizes of Malawi's floral communities can be found. These are the orchids, a group of plants for which Malawi is world renowned. There are in excess of 400 different species across the country, of which a high proportion occur on Nyika Plateau.

The orchids of Malawi include both terrestrial and epiphytic species. The latter grow on living plants, mainly trees, but are not parasitic. Rather, they use their "hosts" as climbing frames or for attachment. One of the problems of plants growing within a forest environment is that light is limited on the forest floor, blocked out by the overhanging canopy of leaves. Their attachment to the uppermost branches of the forest trees enables epiphytic orchids to solve this particular problem and, small as they are, the orchids are able to reap the benefits of living where light is plentiful.

The epiphytic orchids retain the advantages of forest life, however, in that conditions here are often moister than outside the canopy. This is important because the exposed, fleshy roots of the orchids lose water quickly in dry conditions and most epiphytic orchids require the dry season to be tempered by periods of mist and cloud. By contrast, terrestrial orchids, also common on the Nyika Plateau, usually have underground organs in which they store water and nutrients. During the dry season the plants die back, but reshoot after the first rains and soon put out seasonal flowers.

Most orchids in Malawi flower between November and March. Their flowers are not the kind that suffuse whole fields in brilliant splendour, however, and indeed, many of the smaller orchids are not even visible until one is practically upon them, or crouched down beside a stream or tiny crevice. The search is well

worth the effort, however, for their remarkable delicacy and diversity make these plants amongst the most aristocratic of any flora.

If the orchids of Nyika are spectacular on a micro level, it is the wildlife that attracts on a larger scale. The roan antelope (*Hippotragus equinus*) is common on the short grass ranges, while in comic contrast, the ungainly Lichtenstein's harte-beest (*Sigmoceros lichtensteinii*), with the protruding ears and pouting stare of an overgrown teenager, is a less common sight. Numerous other smaller antelope also abound, especially within the reserve itself and, given this abundance of herb-ivores, it follows that predators should also be at least historically abundant on Nyika. Lion and cheetah are occasionally sighted and Nyika boasts the densest leopard population in central Africa.

It is in this highland mixture of grasslands and forest patches that the North Rukuru River rises and begins its steep descent down the western escarpment and into the lake. Cascading over the beautiful Chisanga Falls on the upper plateau, the river turns sharply north here, and plunges through forests and down steep gorges, emerging at last in Lake Malawi. This enormous body of water, with its fascinating diversity of species, is undoubtedly the focus of the region.

The remarkable cichlid

Livingstone referred to Lake Malawi as the Lake of Stars, writing in his journal of the glimmering night sky reflected up from a vast expanse of dark water. He might well have been writing of the bright flashes of colour within the water, however – glimpses of brightly hued cichlid fish for which Lake Malawi is world-renowned.

An estimated 500 species of cichlid fish occur in Lake Malawi, most of which are endemic to this expanse of water. However, it is not just the sheer numbers and colours of cichlid species found in Lake Malawi that attract aquarists, tourists and researchers from throughout the world to this tropical lake. These fish also evince an intriguing array of adaptations towards their environment that, perhaps more than in any other group of animals, has enabled them both to diversify their species numbers and to expand their ranges to occupy virtually every niche with-in the lake, in terms of habitat, feeding and reproduction.

It is in the cichlid group known locally as *mbuna*, or rock fish, that specialisa-tion has occurred to a particularly astounding degree. By developing slight modifications that allow specialisation in certain aspects of their lifestyle, new species evolve in time that are able to occupy unique niches. This specialisation, referred to in scientific circles as adaptive radiation, largely accounts for the unparalleled diversity of species found in the Great Rift Valley lakes, and in Lake Tanganyika, Lake Victoria and Lake Malawi in particular.

It is in terms of their feeding apparatuses that the extent of specialisation of different cichlid species is most apparent. *Mbuna* occur primarily in rocky habitats, and feed on the thick, felt-like material growing on the rock surfaces. This material comprises primarily algae, some of which are attached firmly to the rock in filamentous threads, while others are loosely attached, sometimes single-celled agglomerations. Living within this green microcosm are also bacteria, protozoans and innumerable tiny crustaceans. Together, they form a soft cocktail crust for the *mbuna* hovering above the algal surfaces, and different species have developed a surprising variety of specialisations to enable each one to utilise a slightly different component of the resource.

The small *Pseudotropheus tropheops*, for example, has two rows of small, close-set teeth, the outer row comprising two-pronged teeth while the teeth of the inner row have three prongs. These file-like combinations are used to rasp the algal matting from the rock surfaces, while sharp conical teeth at the edge of the mouth cut through the rasped material. This efficient machinery enables the fish to remove even firmly attached algae from the rocks. Their jaw structure, however, restricts them to feeding on vertical or steeply sloped rock slopes.

By contrast, the inner row of teeth in another *mbuna* species, *Pseudotropheus zebra*, comprises larger, more widely spaced teeth, which allow the fish to comb rapidly over the algal matting, removing the loose material but not the tightly attached filaments. This fish is also restricted to vertical surfaces. Naturally, adaptations towards scraping a meal from horizontal surfaces also abound. *Petrotilapia tridentiger*, for example, has long, curved teeth, flattened and flexible at the tips to allow the algae to be shovelled off the rocks. This is achieved on flat rocks, when the fish hangs vertically in the water, head down over the rock, and shovels its jaw back and forth.

Other *mbuna* have developed similar feeding mechanisms but occupy different depths of the lake. In the generally clear waters of Lake Malawi, light penetrates far enough down to allow algal growth at considerable depths. Its is only in the deepest reaches of the lake, below 200 metres in depth, that the waters are dark and generally devoid of life and movement, save for the constant rain of minute dead plankton that sink slowly to the lake floors from the light and productive surfaces high above.

The development of different feeding traits from single common characteristics is displayed in some of the more anomalous adaptations. Several species of *mbuna* have evolved to scrape less savoury surfaces than algal-matted rocks. *Genychromis mento*, for example, scrapes the body scales from slow-moving bottom dwellers, sometimes extending its preferences to go so far as to remove whole pieces of flesh or fin from its hapless victims as well.

OPPOSITE: *The waters of Lake Malawi lap against the shores of Cape Maclear.*
ABOVE LEFT: *Reeds are able to grow up through the clear lake water.*
ABOVE CENTRE: *Cichlids shoal in the clear deep waters of the lake.*
ABOVE RIGHT: *In the waters closer to the shore at Cape Maclear, shoals of other cichlid species are found, the fish adapted to the particular feeding and habitat conditions of the shallows.*
LEFT: *A cargo of smoked and dried fish, ready to sell in the local markets.*

The overall preference of *mbuna* for a rocky habitat has played an important role in determining the high species diversity of these fish within the lake. Small patches of sand are as restrictive a barrier to the tiny fish – measuring at most some 15 centimetres in length – as whole watercourses, and serve to isolate small groups within a confined area. Here they slowly develop into what are believed to be different species, whilst elsewhere other isolated groups also adapt and develop mechanisms towards exploiting similar resources in a different area. This characteristic explains the fact that some species of *mbuna* are found in only one particular area of the lake, yet occupy habitats that appear to be no different to those found elsewhere.

It is not just the *mbuna* that display specialisations, however. In sheltered sandy or muddy areas, where various eel grasses and other aquatic plants grow in thick profusion, a different suite of cichlids specialise. Here, some species are adapted to sucking algal fronds off the blades of plant material, while others thrive on the rich variety of insect larvae and crustaceans that abound in these sheltered waters. In the sandy zones, by contrast, numerous tiny cichlids feed on the nutritious sediments dropped from the waters above, or on the molluscs, worms or small crustaceans that also inhabit this zone. Like the *mbuna* of the rocky areas, sand dwellers also divide the food and habitat resources into distinct niches, differentiated by the species according to food, depth or sediment type. It is not uncommon for as many as 50 different species of cichlids to breed within a sandy area just a few hundred metres long.

Courtship, breeding and mouth brooding

The breeding habits of cichlids is a topic that warrants attention on its own, for it is in this area of behaviour that these fish display truly bizarre characteristics, including some of the few examples of parental care within any group of fish. During the breeding season – the timing of which varies between different species – the male cichlids establish territories and defend them fiercely. The territories differ in size and definition, from an undemarcated patch of rock, known only to its occupant, to meticulously constructed and carefully maintained nests

LEFT: *The highly adapted lips of this cichlid fish* (Haplochromis labrosus) *allow it to suck small fish and other organisms from within cracks in the rocks.*
ABOVE: *Cichlid fish feed on algal growths on rocks in Lake Malawi.*

FAR LEFT: *Wide enough in places to seem more like a sea than a lake, Lake Malawi stretches out to the horizon.*
ABOVE: *Dugout canoes are traditionally made from hardwood – a rapidly dwindling resource.*
LEFT: *The lake is the sole livelihood of many of the local people, who use these fine fishing nets to haul in their catches.*

in the sand. These nests play an important role during courtship and mating, less for their value as receptacles for eggs than as focal points for the courtship ritual.

Once his territory has been defined and a nest constructed if necessary, the male assumes full breeding colours. Male cichlids are generally more brightly coloured than females, and during the breeding season they can be quite spectacular. Their colours serve both to warn other males away from the territory and to attract females. It has been noted that males leaving their territories to go on food sorties or other expeditions have a mechanism for suppressing their brilliant colouration and thus reducing needless aggression from other males passed by on their route. Once back in the confines of their own territory, however, their bright colours resume their former brazen splendour.

From the male's territory, females of the same species are eagerly solicited, provided they are obviously heavy with eggs and ready to be fertilised. As a female passes a guarded territory, the male treats her to a display of fin quivering, tail twisting and general showing off. If this posturing fails to impress her, she is treated to yet another display of fin-shaking. If any of these performances catch her interest, she follows the male into his territory, and thus begins the second phase of cichlid courtship.

The pair circle closer, nudging each other until the female releases an egg. Instead of merely dropping it into the water to be fertilised, however, she picks it up and holds it in her mouth. This done, she nudges the male's anal fin, prompting him to release sperm into the water. The sperm is breathed in through the female's mouth, where it flows over and fertilises the waiting egg. A few more eggs may be fertilised in the same manner, but the one male is not usually respon-

sible for fertilising a whole brood, and the female moves on, to be solicited by another sex-hungry male.

The fertilised eggs, meanwhile, are kept safe in the female's mouth. Here, protected from predators, they are aerated by the constant stream of fresh water passing through the mouth and over the gills. This process of retaining the eggs and later the young themselves within the mouth until they are old enough to stand a sporting chance of survival, is known as mouth brooding, and is a habit peculiar to almost all of the known Lake Malawi cichlids, with the exception of the redbreast tilapia (*Tilapia rendalli*), which instead lays its eggs in holes in the sand where they are guarded jealously by both parents.

In the female's mouth, the eggs are equipped with a yolk sac, which nourishes the developing fry as they grow. When the yolk sac has been used up, it is time for the fry to obtain their own food. At this stage, the female gently releases them out of her mouth into the water, where they are free to feed on minute planktonic organisms. When danger threatens, the female draws them back into the cavernous safety of her mouth. Female cichlids often congregate in multi-species groups, their young intermingling freely. It is not even uncommon for a female of one species to be found with fry of an entirely different species in her mouth. Of course, as the young slowly increase in size, there is less and less room for them in this refuge and gradually more of them remain outside, until at last the entire brood is fending for itself.

Not all cichlids brood their fry until this stage. Amongst many of the rock-dwelling fish, including the *mbuna*, females look after the fry for a few days only, and then deposit them one by one in crevices and cracks where they will be safe from predation. On the exposed sands, however, where such shelters are scarce, it is more imperative that the young are guarded for a longer period.

Brooding does not, of course, guarantee the safety of the offspring. In fact, it is ironic that this habit has actually led to the evolution of some cichlid species adapted to exploiting the very behaviour aimed at safeguarding the young. These fish, known as brood-robbers or paedophages, specialise in robbing females of their precious cargo of fry by ramming their heads and thus forcing them to eject the shoal of tiny fry housed within, which are then gulped down by the predators.

Other fish of the lake

While cichlids are without doubt the most fascinating of the fish found in Lake Malawi, they are by no means the only fish present there. There are several other families of fish of considerable importance, including the tiny sardine-like *usipa* (*Engraulicypris sardella*), which are heavily fished by local people, as well as several species of carp (of the genus *Labeo*) and the ubiquitous barbel or catfish (of the genus *Clarias*). The latter attain large sizes, and most species are capable of travelling considerable distances overland during the wet season. These feats are enabled by their possession of a secondary breathing apparatus which has led to this family of scaleless fish having an exceptionally wide distribution throughout Africa's waterways. Within Lake Malawi itself, however, one group of catfish, belonging to the genus *Bathyclarias*, has lost this ability for terrestrial navigation and instead occupies a range of specialised niches within the lake, where individuals grow to sizes as large as 30 kilograms, making them the largest fish in the lake. By contrast, another species of catfish grows to only two centimetres in length and weighs but a few grams. This is *Zaireichthys lacustris*, a fish found primarily inside old snail shells that litter the lake bottom.

The degree of speciation found in the fish of Lake Malawi is a reflection of both historic conditions in the lake, over the last tens of thousands of years, and the inherent stability of this enormous body of water. Historically, wetter and drier periods probably led to some areas of the lake being isolated from others. Specialisation occurred in these small areas, which were later merged, when water levels were higher. While these changes probably resulted in diversification over the long term, in the shorter term conditions in Lake Malawi are unlikely to vary dramatically from one year to the next in the lake, and organisms benefit by achieving complete mastery of a particular, narrow niche. By contrast, organisms inhabiting lakes that are prone to short-term desiccation and fluctuations in salinity or oxygen levels, for example, are more likely to survive these vagaries by developing plastic habits, and showing flexibility in their habitat, diet and substrate or depth preferences. Such variable conditions exist in some of the

BOTTOM: *Roots of a* Ficus *tree cling tena-*
ciously to a granite boulder on Momba Island.
BELOW: *Dry summer vegetation grows up*
among massive granite boulders.

PEOPLE OF THE LAKE

For nearly 12 000 years people have been drawn to settle on the shores of Lake Malawi by the gentle climate and the bounty of the lake. The name Malawi is loosely translated as "bright haze", and in the native language of Maravi has connotations of warmth and sunshine, of the glow of sunset or the misty haze of the sun rising over the still waters of the lake.

The earliest known human inhabitants of Lake Malawi were the Pygmy Bushmen, who moved to the lake shores from the forests of the Congo in approximately 10 000 BC. These people were a fierce race, if undeniably short, and legend relates that when greeted by a stranger, their first question was: "From where did you see me when you were coming ?" If the response to this cryptic query was not "I saw you from far away", the stranger was met with a hail of arrows, the implication being that he had dared to say that the Bushman was too short to be noticed from afar.

These aggressive people were followed, in about AD 200, by Bantu-speaking tribes known as the Maravi. This group of people brought with them smelting skills, as well as agriculture and herds of cattle, and today are still the dominant ethnic group in Malawi. Their history has been fraught with violence and trauma, not least of which was the devastating effect wrought by the slave trade during the nineteenth century. Under the terror of Omani slave traders, thousands of people, mainly women and children, were shipped to Zanzibar on the coast to be sold as slaves. In Malawi, this gruesome exercise was given momentum by the co-operation of another more recent arrival of people at the lake: the Yao, many of whom were converted to Islam and assisted the Arabs with their trade in humans, in exchange for weapons.

The shores of the lake have thus witnessed aeons of peace and plenty, as well as bloody massacres and abominations of human rights. Through it all, the lake itself has remained largely unchanged and today — as in the past — the lake forms an integral part of the lives of the people who inhabit its shores and ply its waters. Many Malawians depend on the lake for food, harvesting some 40 000 tonnes of fish from its waters each year. Of these the large *chambo* (*Oreochromis* spp.) is one of the most important species caught.

Fishing is carried out primarily by traditional means, using dugout canoes and handmade nets. The dugouts, or *bwato*, are constructed from local hardwoods, mainly *mtonda*, each craft requiring the trunk of an entire tree. Today the huge trees required to construct the *bwato* are scarce and are sometimes obtained from as far as 50 kilometres inland, where they are first carved out before being transported down to the lake. Once constructed, the *bwato* last some five or six years before becoming waterlogged and too cumbersome for use on the water.

Navigation of these small craft is no mean feat. While they are in fact more stable than they look, the might of Lake Malawi cannot be underestimated. Within a few short minutes, its calm surfaces can change from the languid sheen of a tropical paradise to a heaving mass of white-capped waters driven by furious winds, requiring the skill of an experienced craftsman to ride the storms unscathed.

smaller lakes of Malawi such as Lake Chilwa, in the south. This shallow, inwardly draining or endorheic lake reaches a maximum depth of about three metres during particularly wet years, and often dries out almost completely during drought years. Predictably, therefore, it has few endemic species associated with it.

The lake shore fauna

While the cichlids and other fish are undoubtedly the jewels in Lake Malawi's crown, it would be doing an injustice to dwell entirely on them to the exclusion of the plethora of other wildlife both in and alongside the water. In Lake Malawi National Park – incidentally a park dedicated to the preservation of the *mbuna* – both the Cape clawless otter (*Aonyx capensis*) and the spotted-necked otter (*Lutra maculicollis*) are found. Bringing a more prehistoric atmosphere to the park are the leguaans or water monitors (*Varanus niloticus*), large reptiles that are graceless on land yet move efficiently through the water. They feed on fish and amphibians in the water and small birds and eggs on land.

Lake Malawi is also a haven for the hippo (*Hippopotamus amphibius*) that inhabit the swampy marsh areas and reedbeds along some of the lake shores, adding their grunts and nocturnal roars to the cacophony of insect and amphibian sounds that form a background to the hot summer evenings. Crocodiles (*Crocodylus niloticus*) are also found in the lake, although both hippo and crocodiles occur in much larger densities downstream of the lake, in the Shire River, where reed and marshlands are more common and the shores drop away less steeply. It is for this same reason that birdlife in Lake Malawi, while impressive, is less exciting than that found in the shallows of the rivers, smaller lakes and wetlands, where habitat suitable for wading birds is more abundant. Notwithstanding this, the reedbeds and swamplands fringing parts of the lake offer refuge and feeding grounds to jacanas (*Actophilornis africanus*), glossy and sacred ibises (*Plegadis falcinellus* and *Threskiornis aethiopicus* respectively), and egrets, while several of the smaller islands on the lake are breeding grounds for white-breasted cormorants (*Phalacrocorax carbo*).

TOP: *Zebra graze on the verdant pastures of Nyika Plateau.*
FAR RIGHT: *The Shire Valley – a tropical Eden.*
ABOVE: *A reed frog,* Hyperolius nyika, *finds refuge in the reedbeds that fringe Lake Malawi.*
RIGHT: *Bracken covers the landscape, stretching towards the horizon towards Nyika Plateau.*

The Shire River Valley

South of Lake Malawi, among the wide floodplains of the Shire River with its associated wetlands and marshes, a more luxurious faunal community is found. Downstream of the lake, the river is broad and meandering, with occasional clumps of so-called "floating islands" – massed tangles of reeds and organic debris, pulled free of their rootholds by floods and high waters. These conglomerations drift slowly downstream towards Lake Malombe, the larger ones providing habitat for frogs, birds and sometimes even otters. Eventually, they fall apart or lodge against the river bank and take root.

Hippo and crocodile are as familiar a sight in this area as the reeds and waterways themselves, while terrestrial game thrives on the broad, fertile floodplains where farmland has not eliminated them. These areas are not solely confined to the official national parks of the valley. Regions such as Elephant Marsh on the eastern periphery of the floodplain still remain a haven for a diverse array of wildlife, albeit not the large herds of elephants that once wallowed in the muddy shallows after which it was named. This perennial wetland, set against a backdrop of baobab trees and grassland, holds the largest densities of crocodile in Malawi, as well as large communities of hippo, groups of usually elusive otters and an astounding array of birds. Here, both purple and goliath herons (*Ardea purpurea* and *Ardea goliath*) stand stonily in the shallows, their shadows lost in the movement of reeds and water, while yellow-billed storks (*Mycteria ibis*) and glossy ibises are common in the marsh periphery.

Further downstream, the character of the Shire River changes. Its languid meanders and bird-filled reedbeds give way to a fast-flowing gorge through

which the water roars, pounding over rapids and waterfalls, including the famous Kapichira Falls that blocked Livingstone's first foray up the Shire River in 1859.

Passing out of Lake Malawi, the river carries with it some of the essence of this essentially tropical, barely touched Eden. It remains to be seen, however, for how much longer the influences of humans, with their age-old capacity for wreaking change, can be withstood. As long they are at one with the lake and its biota, however, needing the sustainability of the fauna as an integral part of their lives, there is a chance for this aquatic Eden, once called the "gateway to Africa".

CHAPTER 6

Bwindi: Place of Darkness, Impenetrable Forest, home to
burly mountain gorillas and a plethora of fragile, dusty-winged
butterflies, land of swamps, canopied forest, untouched waterfalls
and loudly rushing rivers. An Eden of immense fragility,
encircled by a growing sea of humanity, where the only chance
of survival is to share the bounty of its diversity.

A mountain gorilla peers through the dense foliage.

Delicate fungi (Crepidotus sp.) fan out from a rotting log.

Impatiens niamniamensis.

Bwindi

UGANDA'S IMPENETRABLE FOREST

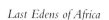

LEFT: *Tree ferns overhanging Munyaga River. This river flows through the catchment of the Ishasha River which, together with the Ivi River, are the two main river systems in Bwindi, providing a source of pure water to the downstream catchment.*
RIGHT: *Bwindi is home to an astonishing diversity of butterflies.*

Bwindi Impenetrable Forest ... the very name exhilarates, awakening long-dormant stirrings for adventure in even the most confirmed of couch potatoes. To visit the forest is to be seduced at once by its astonishing beauty, the luxuriance of its growth forms and its diversity of flora and fauna. Once part of a far more extensive area of rain forest that comprised some 20 per cent of Uganda's land surface, the tiny Bwindi Forest, occupying a mere 331 square kilometres, is virtually all that remains today of Uganda's forest habitat, estimated at less than 2,6 per cent of the country's land surface.

Technically, Bwindi is not in fact a true rainforest, having an average annual rainfall of only about 1 450 millimetres, and is more accurately termed a moist tropical forest. Straddled across the Bwindi Hills in the Rukiga Highlands, lost in the south-western corner of Uganda and surrounded by tea and banana plantations, the Impenetrable Forest rises like an island holding back an encroaching sea of human development.

Despite its size however, the forest supports one of Africa's richest plant and animal communities, numbering more than 350 bird species, 200 tree species, some 350 recorded species of butterflies, numerous other insects, reptiles, amphibians and over 100 mammalian species, with the latter group including over half of the world's population of mountain gorillas. The beauty of the area is thus rivalled only by its tremendous ecological importance, its scientific significance and its economic value as a centre for eco-tourism in Uganda.

The incredible diversity of living organisms found within the Impenetrable Forest can be attributed to the combined influence of several factors. First, the forest encompasses a wide range of physical habitats, being one of the few forests in which a continuum of lowland and montane habitat occur. It is thus able to accommodate a wide range of organisms adapted to fairly narrow altitudinal niches. Similarly, on a horizontal scale, Bwindi's location in the highlands separating the rainforests of the Congo Basin in the west from the savannahs in the east, means that it acts, to a certain extent, as a "mixing zone" for organisms from both these important African biomes, and thus accrues species originating from each. Bwindi's location on the edge of the Albertine Rift Valley, the western extension of the same Great African Rift Valley that resulted in the formation of Lake Malawi, is also a factor in explaining the presence of some species of Bwindi's flora and fauna. The forest is thus home to some of the so-called Albertine Rift endemics, found only in the Albertine Rift Valley itself and the highlands associated with its uplifted western valley.

ABOVE LEFT: *In the moist twilight beneath the forest canopy, trailing lianas, layered with thick lichens and moss, form eerie curtains.*
ABOVE CENTRE: *The pink roots of a young strangler fig reach down for the forest floor, where they will begin taking up food and water of their own and thicken slowly into a deadly knot of roots around their host.*
ABOVE RIGHT: *In a wet ravine, light filtering in through gaps in the canopy and an abundance of moisture have resulted in a dense understorey of lush vegetation.*
LEFT: *Disturbed land at the edge of the forest result in a tangle of impenetrable shrubs, creepers and ground covers.*

Geology and climate

It is perhaps on a geological time scale, however, that the variety of animals and plants still found in Bwindi today, can best be explained. Between 1 000 000 and 25 000 years ago, the gradual expansion of the polar ice-caps resulted in increasing aridity over much of the continent. These climatic changes had a profound influence on the formation of different natural habitats, many of which form the subjects of this book.

The Kalahari thirstlands, for example, resulted from increasing aridity in the interior, while the diversity of the fynbos flora increased dramatically during the same phase, as drought-stressed Afromontane forests retreated into gorges and protected pockets on the mountain sides of the South African Cape Peninsula. Similarly, in the Rukiga Highlands of East Africa, this period saw a retreat of forests into isolated refugia, separated by expanses of grasslands. These refugia were located primarily in the high-lying regions of the area, where altitude coun-

teracted the more arid climate, supplementing meagre supplies of water with relief rainfall and moisture from overhanging clouds.

Within these protected habitats, a large proportion of the natural Afromontane flora and fauna survived the vagaries of climate and, during wetter periods when the forest expanded into the lower areas, these communities acted as pools or "species banks", providing stock with which new areas could be recolonised. Today, Afromontane communities the length of Africa still contain many of the same species, preserved by their altitudinal refuges. No less in the area now occupied by Bwindi Forest, flora and fauna from past millennia have been retained as part of the forest's natural assemblage of species.

Thus today Bwindi encompasses a wide diversity of habitats, from the three-dimensional structure of the forest itself, with its tiered vegetation, to the bamboo thicket of the north east and the range of both upland and lowland swamps, of which Mubwindi Swamp is the largest. Arguably, however, the essence of Bwindi lies in the mystery and magnificence of its forest habitats.

Forest wonderland

From the outside, the forest is truly impenetrable. Vines hang curtain-like between the giant forest trees and here, where light is plentiful, the ground cover is thick and daunting to traverse, save where trails and animal paths already exist. Further in, however, one enters a fairy tale wonderland of dim, green-tinted light, mosses, cascades of ferns and fungi growing over rotting logs, twisting lianas (the woody creepers immortalised by Tarzan films) and the straight trunks of tall forest trees, extending ever upwards to canopies some 40 to 50 metres above the forest floor. In the damp luxuriance of this twilight zone, one can almost hear the whispering of plants, as they twist and twine towards the light.

The availability of light is one of the most important factors in explaining both the structure of the forest and the functioning of its communities. Bwindi itself means Place of Darkness, a fitting term for the heart of the undisturbed, virgin forest, where tall trees create an almost complete canopy across the forest top, absorbing most of the light entering the forest and blocking it off to the plants below. Here, the understorey vegetation comprises ferns, dainty arrangements of bract fungi, small shade-loving perennials, such as plants of the *Impatiens* genus that occur in a variety of shapes and forms throughout the forest, as well as hopeful tree seedlings, growing slowly upwards through the twilight.

Slightly higher up, the middle storey of the forest is occupied by small tree species, and the saplings of taller trees, unable to grow taller until more light becomes available. This happens when one of the taller trees of the forest canopy falls to the ground, thereby creating a gap in the canopy. Like heirs to a throne, many of the middle storey trees will wait many years before a chance to succeed comes their way, if indeed it ever does. In the forest, the most favourable position

for a plant is at the top of the canopy where light is plentiful, and various methods for attaining these heights have been developed by different plant species.

For the large trees, the process is simply one of waiting for a lucky break in the canopy, and growing up to fill it. Some trees, such as the *mukumbwe* tree (*Bosqueia phoberos*) protrude still higher above the canopy, and the sight of their long white trunks rising above the green leaves of the forest is a familiar sight when the forest is seen from afar. For many of the trees of the canopy, however, their immense height means that a normal root system will not provide sufficient support for the top-heavy tree. Many species thus rely on a system of buttressed roots to lend side support to their trunks.

Not all plants are so independent in their search for light, however. Lianas and other climbers grow up from the forest floor, using the strong canopy trees to support their twisting stems. Other groups of plants are still more adept at gaining access to the coveted upper canopy, with a minimum of effort. Epiphytes, including several species of orchids, are a common feature of many of the trees. These plants grow on the branches of tall trees, obtaining their moisture from rain, atmospheric moisture and sometimes from water that accumulates in specially adapted hollow leaves. Nutrients are accessed from the rotting plant material that accumulates around their exposed roots. Planted as seeds by forest birds, the epiphytes find themselves in a position where light is more freely available than on the forest floor, without having to expend energy in getting there.

While most epiphytes benefit from their host plants, without causing actual damage to them, some species have evolved more insidious methods of procuring for themselves suitable positions in the forest hierarchy. These species include the so-called strangler figs, such as *Ficus ottoniifolia*. Birds or forest monkeys eating the fig fruits disperse the seeds in their droppings. By chance, some of these seeds

OPPOSITE: *The sound of dripping, trickling, rushing water forms a constant background to the other forest noises. Here the Munyaga River courses through the forest, pouring over mossy boulders and past fern-lined banks.*
BELOW: *The hollow buttress roots of* Newtonia buchananii, *adapted to support the tall trees in the soft moist forest soils, are used as drums by chimpanzees, which beat out signals to each other across the forest.*

ABOVE LEFT: *The moist, dimly-lit forest floor is an ideal habitat for fungal species such as the dainty* Laschia thwaitsii.
ABOVE CENTRE: *Fairy-tale toadstools push up to the surface, hyphal threads working below to digest and absorb precious nutrients from the decaying leaf litter of the forest floor.*
ABOVE RIGHT: *Many of the plants occurring in Bwindi have local medicinal value. This creeper is used as a cure for stomach cramps. Use of such plants on a controlled and sustainable basis forms part of Bwindi's programme to make the forest an asset and not a competitor to local people.*
LEFT: *Large numbers of caterpillars are found in the lower forest, disguised by hairs, hooks, spines or cryptic colouring, or alternatively, brightly marked to show that they are toxic.*

are caught up amongst the branches in the upper canopy. Here, amply provided with light and moisture, they take root and soon extend clusters of leaves up into the sunlight. At the same time, their long roots grow slowly down towards the ground, penetrate the soil and begin to absorb nutrients. Gradually, the roots thicken into branches and begin to tighten around their host. In time, the tree's stranglehold becomes deadly. The host tree finally dies, its water- and nutrient-carrying vessels cut off, and the fig remains, a tall tree in the prime of the canopy, its trunk forming a permanent shroud around its sacrificial host, its own fruit being in turn consumed in the canopy and possibly dispersed, or falling to the ground far below.

At the foot of the canopy, the forest floor itself is littered with a thick pile of rotting leaves, bark and fallen logs, providing habitat for a suite of decomposers whose role it is to break the material down, releasing nutrients into the soil from where they are eagerly reabsorbed by the thick tangle of roots criss-crossing the forest soil. The process of decomposition in the forest is aided by the warm temperatures and humidity of the forest interior, and recycling of plant material is thus a rapid process.

Creatures of the forest

Overall, the multi-dimensional space of the forest provides habitat for a wide range of animals, and by day, the air reverberates with the explosive shrieks of monkeys and seldom-seen chimpanzees, chirps of frogs, cicadas and crickets and the calls of a rich diversity of bird life. Birds such as the tinker barbet (of the genus *Pogoniulus*) sound all over the forest, their calls reverberating across the valleys like the continuous hammering of metal plates, while occasionally the rhythmic chucks of the bar-tailed trogon (*Apaloderma vittatum*) lead to sightings of this elusive, crimson-chested forest bird.

These animal communities have access to a rich bounty of food within the forest, where the resources are partitioned into different habitats. High in the canopy, different trees flower and fruit throughout the year, providing a year-long resource to the birds of the upper canopy as well as to troops of foraging red-tail monkeys (*Cercopithecus ascanius*) as well as blue monkeys (*Cercopithecus mitis*), rarer black and white colobus monkeys (*Colobus abyssinicus*) and, in some areas, l'Hoest's monkeys (*Cercopithecus l'hoesti*). Much of the produce of the upper canopy falls to the ground, however, where it is consumed by inhabitants of the lower forest. Complex networks of vines and lianas provide highways linking the different levels of the forest and enabling flightless animals, such as snakes and geckos, to pass between habitats, thus allowing them to track the availability of food in different areas.

TOP LEFT: *Vervet monkeys move between the forest canopy and the lower levels, depending on food availability.*
TOP CENTRE: *Dainty blue flowers show bravely on a forest footpath.*
TOP RIGHT: *Given the diversity of forest vegetation, it is not surprising that the diversity of herbivorous insects, such as this camouflaged cricket (family Tettigonidae), is also high.*
ABOVE: *The forest floor, moist, warm and protected from wind, provides a sheltered habitat for an astounding array of delicate flowers.*
RIGHT: *The velvety legs of this sparassid spider propel it silently across the leaf litter on the forest floor.*

While the production of flowers, fruit and seeds in the forest canopy results in it being a sought-after habitat for many animal species, its very exposure to light, from where the bounty springs, is a two-edged sword, for the upper canopy is also highly exposed to predation from above. With leopard exterminated from the forest by hunting activities, the crowned hawk eagle (*Stephanoaetus coronatus*) is one of the larger predators in Bwindi today, and will take monkeys from the upper branches of the canopy. As the shadow of the raptor's wingspan passes overhead, red-tail monkeys set up a fearful shrieking, accentuating their warning alarm by crashing from branch to branch as they swing down from their vulnerable positions in the canopy.

While most of the activity appears at first glance to be taking place high up in the canopy, a careful examination of the forest floor reveals the tell-tale signs of nocturnal or more elusive animals down below. Uprooted tubers in the undergrowth are often the only sign that bush pigs have passed by, while porcupines remain largely out of sight, leaving only the odd abandoned quill as tantalising evidence of their presence.

The elusive elephants of Bwindi

Strangely difficult to glimpse – given their large size – are the elephants of Bwindi. The Impenetrable Forest numbers between 20 and 30 of these magnificent giants. Although the trails they leave are hardly subtle – the passage of a group of elephant through the forest is marked for weeks afterwards by a path of crushed and broken vegetation, muddy pools and trampled wetlands – the elephants themselves are rarely seen. Small herds inhabit the north east of the forest, in the vicinity of the bamboo thickets and Mubwindi Swamp, although some groups wander throughout the forest, restricted only by the steepest slopes.

Surprisingly enough, there exists some doubt as to the actual identity of these forest giants. In general, two subspecies of elephants occur in Africa. The first is the common savannah or bush elephant (*Loxodonta africana africana*), while the second is the less common forest elephant (*Loxodonta africana cyclotis*). Physically, there are clear differences between these subspecies, including the fact that they have different numbers of toenails on their front and hind feet.

Given these somewhat obvious differences, the lack of clear information as to the subspecies of elephant present in Bwindi is surprising, until one ponders the likelihood of anyone having time during an encounter with one of these beasts to enable a thorough examination of its body parts. Many that have encountered them maintain, however, that the Bwindi elephants are in fact bush elephant that have been isolated in the forests for a relatively short period of time.

Whatever their genetic affiliations, large animals such as elephant historically, and to a lesser extent today, played an important functional role in the forest by creating patches of disturbed vegetation within the forest. This augments the rate at which areas of mature forest give way to temporarily disturbed vegetation, not only allowing saplings to grow up and fill the space thus created in the canopy, but also creating a vital habitat type that is utilised by a group of plants that thrive in recently disturbed areas, where light availability is higher. Eventually, these opportunistic communities give way, over long periods of time, first to secondary and then to the so-called "climax" vegetation of the mature forests. Until then, plants such as the herbaceous *Mimulopsis* and species of *Brilliantasia* thrive in the new niche created for them.

Mountain gorillas

To observe a group of mountain gorillas feeding or resting in the shade, impervious to the undisguised curiosity of their less dignified relation, *Homo sapiens*, is an experience that has no parallel. As one stares self-consciously across at their serious, contemplative faces, expressions haughty and seemingly sentient, one has the disturbing feeling that the term *sapiens* might perhaps have better suited this animal than its graceless cousin.

The gorillas of Bwindi are only one of the 10 species of primates found in the forest but, arguably more so than any other forest animal, they have a magnetic appeal of their own. This is probably due to a combination of their immense size, their accessibility to controlled viewing through careful habituation programmes, their endangered conservation status and, perhaps most importantly, to the fascination inherent in encountering a creature so similar to ourselves, but one whose evolutionary history has taken it along such a different path.

Three subspecies of gorilla exist, all confined to the rainforests and moist tropical forests of western and central Africa. Of these, the lowland gorillas are divid-

TOP: *A silverback pauses amidst the saplings and shrubs of a forest clearing. Weighing up to 200 kg, these giant animals had little to fear in their forest habitat before the arrival of man.*

CENTRE: *The damp conditions and abundance of insect prey make the forest floor an ideal habitat for a variety of frogs and toads.*

ABOVE: *The forest provides food and camouflaging habitat to a diverse array of caterpillars. These creatures metamophose at last into the delicate butterflies that throng the forest.*

LEFT: *A mountain gorilla peers implacably out through the thick vegetation at the edge of a clearing.*

CHIMPS OF BWINDI

Yet another claim to fame of the Impenetrable Forest is that it is the only forest in which mountain gorillas and *Pan troglodytes*, the common chimpanzee, are both found. Heard more than seen, however, their raucous hoots echoing through the forest both by day and night, the chimpanzees of Bwindi are far more elusive than the habituated groups of gorillas and, moving through the forest in loose groups, they keep to the arboreal heights in glorious oblivion of those on the ground below.

Unlike the rigid group structure of their more conservative gorilla cousins, chimpanzee groups are controlled by a number of dominant males, which share both the responsibilities of defending the troop and the breeding privileges. A loose hierarchy does exist between the males, however, with those higher up being able to attract more females in oestrus, and thus bearing more young. In general though, males are far more social than females, roaming the forest together and occasionally even forming hunting bands that are able to kill small animals, ranging from nestlings to young bush pigs, with which they supplement their otherwise largely vegetarian diet.

Since most chimp males remain in their natal groups, many of the troop males are related. This is in contrast to the females, which emigrate to other groups on reaching sexual maturity. Chimp females are largely solitary, and have little co-operative interaction with each other. Indeed, a female trying to join a new group is often abused by resident females, and is only likely to succeed in her bid to join if she is able to gain the support and thus the protection of one of the troop males.

Chimp females breed but occasionally, since offspring, if they survive, are only completely weaned at about six years of age. When females do come into oestrus, however, they are eagerly competed for by sex-hungry males. Despite the apparently liberal sex lives of chimps, however, breeding is a business requiring at least a degree of commitment from both partners. Few chimp pregnancies thus result from "one-night stands" and in the majority of cases, a receptive female and her selected mate disappear together into the forest on so-called "chimp honeymoons", where they remain together for the female's entire oestrus period.

ed into two distinct subspecies, namely the western lowland gorilla (imaginatively christened *Gorilla gorilla gorilla*) found in the lowland rainforests of Congo, Democratic Republic of Congo (formerly Zaire), Cameroon and Gabon, and the eastern lowland gorilla (*Gorilla gorilla graueri*) found in the forests of eastern Democratic Republic of Congo. Populations of these two subspecies are still relatively high (approximately 20 000 of the former, and an estimated 3 000 of the latter), although the combined effects of loss of habitat and hunting are resulting in a frightening drop in their populations. When compared to populations of the third gorilla subspecies, however, the mountain gorillas, whose population numbers approximately 600 animals in total, these figures appear positively robust.

The mountain gorilla (*Gorilla gorilla berengei*) today occurs in a highly restricted area, with almost half of its population being found within Bwindi Forest, while the rest roam the Virunga Mountains, between Congo, Rwanda and the Mgahinga Gorilla National Park in southern Uganda.

Today, some 28 groups of mountain gorillas are estimated to occur in Bwindi Forest, numbering between two and 23 animals per group. On a superficial level, their lives appear idyllic. Rising from nests on the ground when they are warm enough to feel comfortable, and sleeping in when rain and cloud cool down the temperatures in the forest, groups of these lazy wanderers divide their day between alternate bouts of feeding, sleeping and wandering on to new browsing areas.

Equipped with only a simple one-roomed stomach, incapable of completely digesting the fibrous vegetation comprising the bulk of their diet, gorillas have to consume large quantities of food in order to extract sufficient energy for their daily needs. An adult male will thus eat about 20 kilograms of food each day, and the

inefficiency of their digestive systems is demonstrated by their bloated stomachs and the constant symphony of belches and gaseous releases from their nether regions, characteristic of a contented group of gorillas. In addition to feeding on vegetation, gorillas supplement their diets with insects, soil and dung, to compensate for the low levels of Vitamin B12, potassium and calcium in their diets.

In terms of vegetation, they consume a wide variety of different plants, depending on the availability of different species within their home ranges. Despite the local variation in plants, however, adult gorillas are generally highly conservative about their diets, and resist experimenting with new food sources. In fact, it is only young gorillas that are responsible for the addition of new plants to the group's diet. At around two years of age, gorilla juveniles explore their surroundings with a curiosity akin to that of human babies, putting different items into their mouths, some of which are edible, some harmful, and some, such as stones, just inappropriate. When new plants are found to be edible, however, they may be added to the group's list of acceptable foodstuffs.

Each group of gorillas is led by a dominant male, known as the silverback – a name derived from the fact that when male gorillas mature at around 15 years of age, a band of their back hair turns a distinctive silver colour. The largest of all primates, silverbacks tower above the rest of their family, their immense size an evolutionary adaptation to their role as defenders of the group. These groups are, for the most part, stable, cohesive units, comprising mature females, juveniles and immature females and males, the latter known as blackbacks.

THIS PAGE: *Butterflies gather at the edge of a small damp patch, and begin furiously applying their proboscises onto the substrate. Known as "mud-paddling", this curious display actually allows them to extract precious salts and minerals, concentrated at the edge of a puddle, or on piles of animal dung or urine. Possessing a mechanism that allows them to extract these substances even when at extremely low concentrations, the butterflies cycle large quantities of liquid through their bodies, removing what minerals they can.*

Although occasionally the presence of a second mature male, the son or sibling of the dominant silverback, is tolerated in the group, breeding privileges are reserved entirely for the group leader, who mates with his bevy of breeding females. These females are ranked socially in terms of their age, the number of young they produce and their current position of favour with the silverback. At times, lone silverbacks, or those with small groups, will succeed in attracting a low-ranked female from a larger, established group to join them. For a female, moving to a smaller group can be a quick way of rising up the gorilla social hierarchy, and, for a sixth- or seventh-ranked female in one group, the option of becoming a first- or second-ranked female in a smaller group is likely to appear attractive.

In terms of gorilla group dynamics, such between-group migrations are a simple way of allowing mixing of group genes. Indeed, most females leave their natal groups in this manner, shortly after reaching sexual maturity between seven and nine years of age. They may change groups several times during their lives, but, in general, remain faithful to a group once they have bred there. Young males also leave their natal groups, wandering the forest alone until they are able to attract females to join them. In this manner, destructive physical conflict over females between rival males is largely avoided, and silverbacks of different groups usually confine their aggression to vocal threats and mock charges, while the females quietly decide to leave one group and join another.

Direct take-overs of an entire group are thus rare, although when they do occur, they are violent and bloody. A rival silverback intent on possession of a group of females must first kill or drive away its current lord. Armed with ferocious canines and vicious claws, such confrontations are terrifying to behold. Moreover, if the interloper is successful in his challenge, the battle is followed by bloody carnage, as all offspring belonging to his predecessor are killed. This action ensures not only that in future all offspring in the group will be the product of the new male, but the loss of their young serves to bring mature females of the group back into oestrus very quickly, and the new silverback can begin producing his own offspring within a short period of time. Such take-overs within a group are rare, however, and it is more common for a silverback to lead his group well into old age, and often until he dies.

Throughout his period of leadership, the silverback fathers all offspring born to his group. While he tolerates sexual play between other males and females of the group, when a female is in oestrus only he is allowed to mate her, a process which is accompanied by a series of loud, satisfied copulatory calls. The fact that all offspring in the group belong to the silverback means that he can also afford to show interest in their upbringing, without risking perpetuating the genes of a rival silverback. Thus juveniles often interact closely with the silverback, and this stern-looking patriarch responds to their clumsy handling with surprising gentleness. Indeed, silverbacks have on occasion even been known to adopt juveniles whose mothers have died.

Creatures great ... and small

While the mountain gorillas are undoubtedly the most evocative and emotionally appealing of the Bwindi fauna, no account of the Impenetrable Forest would be complete if it rested with them alone. Indeed, easily the most conspicuous and arguably the most beautiful of the forest fauna is actually the incredibly diverse assortment of butterflies found there. As one walks along paths or through forest clearings, flocks of brightly coloured butterflies rise in soft profusion off the ground, their wings merging in a mass of colours and different markings, making it easy to believe the statistic of over 350 butterfly species being recorded there thus far.

In fact, the butterfly population of Bwindi is among the most diverse in Africa. This is largely because of the factors already discussed in this chapter, such as the altitudinal range encompassed by the forest, which contributes to the overall species diversity within the forest. In addition, the existence of a diverse range of vegetation types has resulted in increased diversity of habitat and dietary material, thus further encouraging the presence of a wide and diverse range of butterfly species within the forest.

Hundreds of grass-whites and yellows of the family Pieridae flutter weakly in the faded sunlight of forest clearings, while above, the jagged-winged charaxes (members of the subfamily Charaxinae), adapted to powerful flight, remain largely in the canopy, lured to the forest floor only occasionally by the strong odours of rotting fruit and piles of animal dung. Attracted by the alcohol produced by fruit, the drinking habits of these butterflies cause them on occasion to lose their powerful flying style and weave drunkenly from plant to plant, until the effects of their last liquid intake have worn off.

Closer to the ground, brightly patterned acraeas (Acraeinae subfamily) can afford their slow, leisurely flight across the forest floor, their distinct markings advertising to all would-be predators that they contain toxins (in most cases, cyanide compounds) and should not be considered further on the menu. In the shaded vegetation, the iridescent blue of forest mother of pearls (*Salamis temora*) shine luminously out of the foliage, while the velvet browns of junonias (*Junonia* genus) remain unseen, until the movement of their wings fanning slowly open and closed alerts one to their presence amongst the rotting surface debris.

LEFT: *The Bizenga River, a tributary of the Munyaga River. The numerous waterways of Bwindi play an important role beyond the boundaries of the forest, with Bwindi serving as the primary source of water for Lake Edward, in the Rift Valley north and west of the forest.*

CHAPTER 7

Madagascar: a biological and cultural melting pot, one-time home to a pygmy hippopotamus and the largest bird that ever lived; now the haunt of rare lemurs and chameleons, a paradise of rainforest, coral reefs and idyllic bays... Land of awesome and savage beauty, millions of years of adaptation and change have resulted in the astonishing diversity still found there today.

A nest fern in Montagne d'Ambre.

Young Antakarana girl.

Stalactites and stalacmites in a cave in Ankarana.

Parson's chameleon.

Madagascar

NOAH'S ARK OF THE INDIAN OCEAN

LEFT: *The paradise island of Nosy Mangabe.* **RIGHT:** *A snake* (Madagascaraophis colubrinus) *swallows a gecko.*

Madagascar is sometimes referred to as a mini-continent, so diverse are its landscapes and ecosystems and so large is its size. Like the islands of the Seychelles, it has long fascinated biologists and evolutionists for the remarkable examples it contains of adaptive radiation. Over millions of years, and subsequent to the process of continental drift, many species of animal and plant have taken an evolutionary course that is unique; indeed, the vast majority of its species are found nowhere else in the world. Among these, the lemurs and chameleons are some of the most fascinating, and new species of plants and animals are still being discovered.

The island is astonishing not only for the endemicity of its species and their extraordinary variety, but for the awesome and often savage beauty of its landscapes. From the tropical rainforest of the Masoala Peninsula and the idyllic Baie d'Antongil with its paradise island of Nosy Mangabe, to the spectacular mountain stronghold of Montagne d'Ambre and the forbidding network of underground tunnels and caves at the limestone fortress of Ankarana, Madagascar still has all the ingredients of a Garden of Eden. Yet, like the other last wild places of Africa, the fragility of its position is painfully clear, and the inevitable swathe of destruction that follows human population is already taking its tragic toll.

Geology and topography

Some 250 million years ago, Pangea, the original landmass on earth, began its gradual break-up into two supercontinents, Gondwanaland and Laurasia. The process was a slow one, even in a geological time frame, and it took many millions of years for the earth's major land masses to finally separate from one another. Over the next 65 million years the enormous southern portion, Gondwana, gradually drifted northward, losing large sections such as Antarctica and Australia along the way.

The precise geological relationship between Africa, India and Madagascar remains controversial, but available geological evidence indicates that, before the supercontinent broke apart about 180 million years ago, Madagascar was a continental fragment of Greater India which attached to Africa in the vicinity of present-day Ethiopia. As India started to drift northward, a large chunk of land broke away from Africa during the Jurassic quiet zone, about 165 million years ago, and slowly drifted eastward, away from Africa and into the Indian Ocean. It ceased relative motion about 45 million years later, and today is known as Madagascar.

Madagascar is the fourth largest island in the world, after Greenland, New Guinea and Borneo. Although dwarfed by the African mainland, the island is about 1 580 kilometres long and about 570 kilometres at its widest point, giving it an area of 590 000 square kilometres – approximately the same size as France and a little smaller than Texas.

The size and latitudinal span of the island gave rise to great variations in climate. The island can be divided roughly into several broad zones. One is the high

ABOVE: *Known as the cathedral, this large cave originated where a large section of the roof collapsed on an underwater river. The rays of the sun reach the floor briefly only during the middle of the day.*
FAR LEFT ABOVE: *The sharp lime-stone spikes of the "tsingy" are the result of millions of years of leaching.*
ABOVE CENTRE: *Numerous species of amphibians and reptiles can be seen during the wet season in the forests that surround Ankarana. Here, a snake, (Madagascarophis colubrinus) eats a frog on the forest floor.*
FAR LEFT: *Lac ver, or Green Lake, lies high in the Ankarana massif. It is fed by rain and underwater rivers.*
LEFT: *Giant land snails mate on the forest floor in Ankarana. These animals are hermaphrodite and the male and female reproductive ducts are clearly visible.*
OPPOSITE: *Ankarana comprises a large massif of Jurassic limestone traversed by rivers and canyons.*

plateau, or *haut plateaux*, situated on a chain of mountains that runs like a spine along the length of the island, reaching 2 876 metres at its peak on Maromokotro mountain in the north. The high plateau consists mostly of expanses of grasslands that can be exeedingly cold and bleak in winter, with snow occasionally falling in the higher areas.

In the central regions of Madagascar, the monotony of the grasslands is broken by impressive granite domes. Along the eastern side of the country, the high plateau tapers off into a coastal plain, with what were naturally once the dense montane forests of the eastern slopes of the plateau giving way to the lush and humid tropical forests of the plains. The western coastal plains are wider than those in the east, but also drier, and deciduous forests and grasslands are the principal form of vegetation. The south is dry, and here the characteristic vegetation is known as "spiny forest".

Other impressive landscapes include the limestone karst in the north-western part of the country. Locally known as the *tsingy*, after the sound the limestone pinnacles make when hit with an object, this landscape of pinnacles, caves, potholes and underground rivers is truly unique.

Fauna and flora

Madagascar is separated from Africa by the Mozambique Channel and at the nearest point is about 400 kilometres away from the mainland. Like an ancient Noah's Ark, Madagascar took with it a large complement of species into evolutionary exile. Largely undiluted by genetic infusion from the African mainland, these life forms evolved into a unique set of plants and animals. It is not only the isolation from the mainland, however, that caused new life forms to evolve. Being a large island, Madagascar itself consists of many different types of environments, including dry landscapes, rainforests and high plateaux, to name but a few. The biological survivors of the great breakaway from Africa are those that successfully adapted to the new environmental constraints that were imposed on them.

Thus, over a period of many millions of years, adaptive radiation took place on a spectacular scale, resulting in the unique fauna and flora found on Madagascar, approximately 90 per cent of which species today are found nowhere else in the world. Many of them have features that are recognisable in their counterparts on the African mainland, while others have the appearance of creatures from a

ABOVE: *The Madagascar ground boa* (Acrantophis madagascariensis) *is the largest snake in Madagascar and can reach as long as 3 metres. It hunts mainly at night, eating small mammals, including lemurs.*
FAR LEFT: Brookesia stumpffi, *a miniature ground-dwelling chameleon that is able to change colour with remarkable speed.*
LEFT: *The damp forest floor in the vicinity of the caves provides an ideal habitat for crabs that feed on decaying plant material.*

fantastical fairytale world. Some belong to relic lineages that exist elsewhere only in the fossil record, while others can be considered the living representatives of ancient ancestors that gave rise to present-day groups of animals such as the primates. The most famous of these are the lemurs, regarded as "primitive" by biologists because they share characteristics with early ancestral primates.

Primates: ancient to modern

Long before the dinosaurs disappeared from the earth, the earliest ancestors of the mammals were slowly becoming distinct from the other reptiles through natural selection. Very early on in this splitting-off process a line of insectivorous shrews, known today only from the fossil record, took to the trees in Africa – a step that allowed them to escape from predators that roamed at ground level. These arboreal shrews were probably similar to modern-day shrews in that they had a keen sense of smell, good hearing that distinguished effectively between different pitches, and a fine sense of balance. From the fossil record we know that these ancient shrews gave rise to a group of descendants, the lemuroids, most of which retained less specialised hands and feet than other groups of primates. They did,

however, evolve long bushy tails that aided their sense of balance, especially as they jumped from branch to branch or tree to tree. The ancient tree shrews also developed even more keen vision, aided by a shift in the position of the eyes from the sides of the head to the front, thus enabling objects to be seen by both eyes at once. From here developed stereoscopic vision – a process whereby images from each eye are processed to allow accurate judgements of the relative distance of objects. The advantages of this evolutionary step are obvious, considering that the lemur's survival depends on accurately catching a branch as it leaps.

The ancient tree shrews eventually gave rise to three broad groups of primates: the prosimians (or "pre-monkeys"), the monkeys and the hominids, which include the large apes and humans. By the time these groups were becoming distinct about 36 million years ago, Madagascar had already drifted away from Africa. The Mozambique Channel would have been a formidable barrier for the early lemurs to cross, and current thinking is that they made their way across the channel on branches that floated down swollen rivers and were washed out into the sea. This theory is not as unlikely as it may sound at first. Flooding is a common occurrence along the tropical coast of eastern Africa, and many flooded rivers flow directly into the Mozambique Channel.

ABOVE: *Thousands of insectivorous bats fly out of a gorge in Ankarana on their way to feed for the night.*
FAR LEFT: *A male crowned lemur* (Eulemur coronatus).
CENTRE: *The rufous form of the Madagascar paradise flycatcher* (Terpsiphone mutata) *on its nest.*
LEFT: *Antakarana woman dressed for a religious ceremony that celebrates the delivery of her people from the warriors of the highlands.*

Other animals and plant life

The same adaptive radiation that is evident in the lemurs is also present in other groups of animals. Madagascar has about 250 species of bird, of which over 100 are endemic to the island. Despite the mobility that allows them to migrate over long distances, more than 150 types of bird species breed only on Madagascar. Various groups of birds display the same adaptive radiation that Charles Darwin recorded for finches in the Galapagos archipelago. The different species have evolved a variety of morphological and behavioural adaptations, including spanning a wide size range and a diverse array of food items.

Reptiles and amphibians are much less mobile than birds, making the degree of endemicity found on Madagascar still more astonishing. The country has some 500 species of reptiles and amphibians and about 98 per cent of them occur only there. Over half of the world's chameleon species occur on Madagascar and new species are still being discovered. The island is home to both the smallest and largest chameleons in the world, the pygmy stump-tailed chameleon (*Brookesia minima*), which is about twice the size of a thumbnail, and Parson's chameleon (*Calumma parsonii*) which can be well over half a metre long, including the tail.

Although the island is equivalent to just two per cent of Africa's land mass, it supports almost one-fifth of the continent's vascular plants, over 85 per cent of which are endemic to Madagascar. Orchids alone account for more than 1 000 of these species, the different species being easily distinguished by their size or colour. *Cymbidiella rhodochila* has clusters of flowers up to 10 centimetres in diameter, yellow-green in colour and decorated by large green spots. The comet orchid, *Angraecum sesquipedale*, produces spectacular white flowers between July and September. This species was made famous by Charles Darwin, who marvelled at how any insect could have a proboscis long enough to pollinate the 30 centimetre flower. Orchid flowers are pollinated by birds, insects and even geckos, who come to lick the nectar and pollen and carry it on to other flowers. The degree of specialisation and coevolution between plant and pollinator is so great that sometimes only one animal species has evolved the equipment necessary to exploit nectar and pollen and fertilise the flower.

The forests also contain many species of palms, ferns and bamboo, one of the most famous of which is the ravinala palm (*Ravinala madagascariensis*), the national emblem of Madagascar. Resembling a banana tree from afar, this palm has a beautiful fan-shaped rosette of large flattened leaves arranged in a semi-circle above the stem. It is also known as the traveller's palm, both because it stores water in the base of its leaf stalks, a boon for exhausted travellers, and because it is reputed that the plant aligns itself along an east-west axis, providing direction for those who are lost. The latter inference is not, however, strictly true.

The drier regions of the island also contain seven or eight species of baobab (as opposed to only one species in Africa), as well as plants of succulent and spiny genera such as *Aloe* and *Didiera*. There are also other species adapted for dry conditions, such as the nine species of the genus *Pachypodium*, commonly known as elephant's foot.

Paradise under pressure

It is believed that people first came to Madagascar between 1 500 and 2 000 years ago. The first inhabitants were probably from Malaysia and Polynesia, while later arrivals included slaves and settlers from Africa. These early ancestors brought with them the rice and cattle that were integral to their diet and culture in their respective lands of origin. Even later arrivals included traders, mostly of Indian, Chinese, Arabian and Portuguese origin, and French colonists.

Thus, just as in the case of its biological evolution, Madagascar became a melting pot for several different cultures. The Malagasy language spoken today itself evolved from the Austronesian family of languages, which includes among others Indonesian and Polynesian languages and dialects, and it is thought that the closest linguistic relationship to Malagasy is found in languages spoken today in southern Borneo.

RIGHT: *This crystal clear stream on Nosy Mangabe is purported to have healing powers. People come from far away to bathe in it.*
FAR RIGHT: *The roots of pristine mangroves that fringe the coast of the Masoala Peninsula are exposed at low tide.*
BELOW: *Tampolo marine reserve on the Baie d'Antongil is one of the first official coastal reserves in Madagascar and one of the few places where rainforest meets coastal reef.*

ABOVE CENTRE: *The Madagascar tree boa* (Sanzinia madagascariensis) *has heat-sensitive pits around its upper and lower lips to help detect warm-blooded prey.*
ABOVE: *The nymph of the snout beetle, regarded as a delicacy by the local people.*

Not surprisingly, the arrival of people had an enormous impact on the ecology of the island. Although its existence was reported by Marco Polo and the island was already known to Arabian cartographers, the first Europeans arrived in 1500 as a Portuguese fleet under the command of Diego Dias. By then a great many spectacular animals had already disappeared from Madagascar, including about 15 species of lemur, one as large as a human being, a pygmy hippopotamus and the elephant bird, in all probability the largest bird that ever lived. This bird, *Aepyornis maximus*, was bigger than the African ostrich and stood about 2,4 to 2,7 metres tall, weighing perhaps as much as 450 kilograms. Fragments of its enormous eggs lie uncovered on the plains of the drier southern part of the island.

Masoala Peninsula – the Garden of Eden

The Masoala Peninsula is located in north-eastern Madagascar. It is a large, pear-shaped landmass that juts out into the Indian Ocean and is home to the largest remaining tropical rainforest in Madagascar. It contains over 200 000 hectares of primary rainforest, which includes lowland humid forest as well as cloud forest that grows along the upper slopes of the 1 000 metre high mountain chain running along the peninsula's western side. The deep interior of this forest is pristine and not many trails are found there.

On the eastern side, the shoreline of the peninsula is protected from the open sea by a barrier reef that runs along the shore, sometimes several kilometres away from the beach, thus creating large lagoons between the reef and the land. Within these lagoons are splendid coral gardens, as well as an astonishing variety of tropical creatures. Beyond the reef lies the open sea – a wide, blue expanse that stretches into the distance, towards Australasia.

From the air the Masoala Peninsula appears to be covered by many kilometres of giant green blanket with an uneven surface. The forest canopy is so dense and continuous that a passenger in a light aircraft is not afforded even a glimpse of the secret world that exists beneath, except of course in those places where the rivers are wide enough for trees not to touch one another across the vast expanse of water.

Walking through the forest is an unforgettable experience. The tall trees in the primary forest, which support the canopy some 30 metres above the forest floor, are overgrown by mosses and epiphytes that grow high above the ground on other plants in an attempt to reach the sunlight. The branches of the large trees are draped with lianas. While the sun beats down on the canopy from above, only some of its rays filter through to the world below, so that the primary forest is cool and dark and the undergrowth relatively open. The floor of the forest is covered with a thick layer of leaf-litter that is usually damp, even in the dry season. At night, smells from various flowers drift through the forest on the breeze and the movements of millions of fireflies unexpectedly describe exotic three-dimensional dance patterns in the space between heaven and earth. Many other species abound here; the forest is also home to two of the world's rarest birds, the serpent eagle (*Eutriorchis astur*) and the Madagascar red owl (*Tyto soumagnei*).

The Baie d'Antongil and Nosy Mangabe

The west side of the Masoala Peninsula borders an idyllic bay, known as the Baie d'Antongil, one of the few breeding places of the humpback whale in the western Indian Ocean. During the winter months, large numbers of these gentle creatures and their young congregate in the bay, along with dolphins, turtles and a range of other marine creatures. The Baie d'Antongil also contains one of the true jewels of Madagascar: an archipelago of small islands, the largest of which is Nosy Mangabe. This island lies about 4 kilometres from the town of Maroantsetra, which is located at the mouth of the Antainambalana River.

With its golden sandy beach, Nosy Mangabe has all the components of a paradise island. Covered by rainforest, the slopes of the island rise sharply to about 331 metres, and from this height there are spectacular views in all directions. The animals on the island are relatively tame, and there are a variety of orchid species and other flowering plants. As the island is now a national park, one can drink from the numerous crystal clear streams without fear of disease. There are several indigenous fish species and a variety of invertebrates, as well as several large skinks of the genus *Amphiglossus*. At the least sign of danger, these lizards slide into the water and hide between the rocks or in the leaf-litter at the bottom of the creeks.

Nosy Mangabe's protected location at the top end of the Baie d'Antongil made it an ideal refuge for Dutch pirates several centuries ago. From the island they could control the bay relatively easily and, being near the mainland, they were able to restock their supplies. Today, the names of some of these pirates remain engraved in rock on the island.

Halfway to the summit of the island is a cave that functions as a tomb for several families from the mainland. Ancestor worship is common in traditional

RIGHT: *Weaving products in a market at Maroantsetra.*
CENTRE: *Clear seas cover the corals in a lagoon on the Masoala Peninsula.*
FAR RIGHT: *A leaf-tailed gecko (Uroplatus fimbriatus) assumes a threatening posture.*
BELOW LEFT: *Dugout canoes are used for fishing and are also the main form of inshore transport around the Masoala Peninsula.*
BELOW CENTRE: *A catch of reef fishes.*
BELOW RIGHT: *The land hermit crab (Coenobia sp.) is a common inhabitant of the coastal areas of Madagascar.*

Malagasy society, and bones of the deceased are commonly exhumed several years after the death of the person, in a ceremony during which the living commune with their ancestors. Finally, the bones are wrapped in cloth and put in small coffins made of stone and concrete. Several of these coffins and the exposed bones of ancestors can still be seen in this cave, where they lie protected from rain.

The word *manga* in Malagasy refers both to the mango fruit and the colour blue. It is likely that Nosy Mangabe is named after the bluish-green tint of the forested hills of the island, literally translating to "the great blue-green".

Nosy Mangabe contains large numbers of one of the most striking examples of natural selection that exists on the planet. Locally known as *taha*, the species *Uroplatus fimbriatus*, the largest of the leaf-tailed geckos, has a pattern that resembles the bark of a tree. Its tail is flat and when resting the animal often assumes an upside-down position, its body flattened against the surface of a tree. A frill of skin around its jaw and torso breaks the outline of the animal and helps it to blend perfectly into the background. When camouflage fails, the animal can become agitated, opening its mouth wide and threatening the intruder with a bright red tongue and the prospect of a pinch-like bite. There are about 10 species of *Uroplatus*, all of which rely on near-perfect camouflage in a variety of habitats.

The island also supports five lemur species, of which the black-and-white-ruffed lemur *Varecia variegata variegata* and the white-fronted brown lemur (*Eulemur*

fulvus albifrons) are common. The most remarkable of all lemurs, the aye-aye (*Dubentonia madagascariensis*), has also been successfully re-introduced here. This elusive, nocturnal lemur is seldom seen. It appears part lemur, part rodent, has bat-like ears and a grizzled appearance on account of its white-tipped black fur. As bizarre as it is frightful in its appearance, the aye-aye is regarded with great awe by local villagers, who consider the animal a harbinger of death. The aye-aye has a skeletal middle finger, which it uses to hook grubs from the bark of trees and allows the animal to occupy a niche similar to that of the woodpecker in Africa.

Where coral reef meets rainforest

The Masoala Peninsula is one of the few remaining places where large sections of pristine rainforest still meet coral reef. The western side of the peninsula has steep slopes and many of them have escaped deforestation for that reason. Tall green trees draped with lianas grow right up to edge of the beach, and beyond a thin strip of golden sand lies the crystal clear water of the bay. Although the Baie d'Antongil has no barrier reef, there are significant coral deposits that rival the most beautiful anywhere in the Western Indian Ocean.

In both the coral reef and the rainforest – two parallel worlds of extraordinary diversity that exist alongside one another – the forces of natural selection are driven by processes such as predation. The inhabitants of both systems have evolved superb camouflage and other mechanisms of deception to escape predation.

Pressure on the reef by local fishermen is growing and foreign fishing vessels regularly plunder the Baie d'Antongil. Three marine reserves were delimited four years ago, but the foreign NGOs in charge of project Masoala have been slow to develop local capacity to manage the reserves. Consequently, much-needed progress toward establishing sustainable resource use patterns have been seriously impeded. It is essential that projects such as this one focus on promoting environmental education and developing the capacity of the inhabitants to manage their resources themselves. Unless a strong sense of ownership is instilled in the local people, the chances of these resources surviving are slim indeed.

Northern Madagascar

The extreme north of Madagascar consists mostly of rather open deciduous forest that has the appearance of African savannah, complete with baobab trees and rocky outcrops. Beyond this scenic landscape lie wide expanses of blue ocean, and several bays dotted with islands. Near the northernmost tip is the bustling city known as Diego Suarez or Antsiranana, which is a springboard for two of Madagascar's greatest natural wonders further south: the cloud forest of Montagne d'Ambre, about 30 kilometres south, and the ancient limestone fortress of Ankarana.

Island in the clouds

Montagne d'Ambre, meaning Amber Mountain, is a prominent volcanic massif which at an altitude of 1 475 metres and with an average rainfall of about 3,5 metres, is effectively an island of rainforest that towers above the much drier plains. The top of the mountain is frequently veiled in swirling cloud, and the lushness of the forest makes it a suitable habitat for a variety of typical rainforest creatures, including leaf-tailed geckos, lemurs and a range of amphibians. It is also home to about 70 bird species, including the crested wood ibis and the malachite kingfisher. A number of rivers snake through the forest and cascade over waterfalls, some of them 80 metres high, wending their way down the mountain to feed the surrounding plains. At least one of these rivers connects Montagne d'Ambre with the ancient limestone massif of Ankarana that lies further south. Several craters form beautiful blue lakes in a landscape of unbroken green forest. Today much of the rainforest is protected as a national park.

An ancient limestone fortress

From a distance, the limestone massif of Ankarana rises above the plains as a giant monolith of greyish-black rock. Surrounded by mostly sandy soils that support semi-deciduous forest land, the massif is an ecological island of rock that can best be described as pinnacle karst. The range is about 28 kilometres long and 8 kilometres wide. The dark massif is traversed by deep, straight fault-controlled canyons. Few of the canyons are less than 10 metres wide, while some are wider than 50 metres. Their sides are usually vertical and most of them have caves that lead deep into the mountain's interior. These deep furrows are extremely impressive from the air and several of them make it possible for vast, crocodile-infested rivers to flow through the massif on their way to the sea.

The exact origin of Ankarana is not certain. According to one theory it was a giant coral reef at a time when the land was covered by water, and many marine fossils embedded in the limestone would seem to substantiate this. The surface of the rock is covered by extremely sharp pinnacles caused by many millions of years of leaching. These pinnacles make the mountain virtually impassable, and it is only with the greatest difficulty and in certain places that one can ascend the rock walls and traverse the summit of the mountain. This can be an extremely dangerous undertaking, as the mountain is hollow in places and there is a possibility of the roof of the caves collapsing and causing a deadly fall into the crevices below.

As one approaches the mountain, the gaping mouths of the caves are visible from several kilometres away. Utterly forbidding to the less adventurous, these entrances lure biologists and speleologists to explore the dark, unseen world inside the mountain. The caves contain unique biota, including endemic prawns

OPPOSITE TOP: *One of the water-filled craters in Montagne d'Ambre, or "Amber Mountain".*
FAR LEFT: *The rainforest of Montagne d'Ambre is often shrouded in clouds, providing an ideal environment for plants such as ferns.*
ABOVE RIGHT: *A slug feeds on leaves in the rainforest. These molluscs do not have shells, but are protected by a slimy, leathery surface.*
ABOVE LEFT: *Pandanus is one of the more striking plant species found in Montagne d'Ambre.*
LEFT: *The strangler fig uses other plants for support, encircling its host in a stranglehold and eventually killing it.*

and blind fish, and traverse the insides of the mountain in a network of passages that may well cover several hundreds of kilometres. In fact, over 140 kilometres of cave have already been recorded, but experts suspect that the total length of passages inside the bowels of the mountain may well be double that figure.

In the massif a number of impressive collapses are clearly visible from the air. The biggest one is Mangihy, which is almost a kilometre long, about 600 metres wide and 100 metres deep. These collapses form deep depressions in the mountain in which sunken forests are embedded, many of which are isolated from the outside world by the forbidding landscape of spines and spires or accessible only through a network of caves. In some cases, the sunken forests have several cave openings leading from them, making the possibilities for exploration endless.

The mountain is surrounded by a ring of dense forest, fed by both water running off the rock surfaces and underground rivers that flow out of the mouths of many of the caves during the wet season, between December and May. This forest and the deep, forested canyons that traverse the massif, are thought to contain the highest density of primates of any forest in the world, including at least seven species of lemur.

Other mammals that inhabit the forest include the Madagascar ring-tailed mongoose (*Galidia elegans*), for example, is as elegant as its name implies. Living in small groups of three or four, these elongated and sleek reddish-brown animals slink around the forest understorey and along the branches of fallen trees with the greatest of ease. The nucleus of the group is a male and female that pair for life, and they are accompanied by their young and previous set of offspring. They eat a variety of prey and are also thought to occasionally take small lemurs.

The most remarkable of the island's carnivores occurs in Ankarana. Known as the *fosa* (*Cryptoprocta ferox*), it has characteristics of both the dog and the cat family. In fact it belongs to neither, but to the family Viverridae, which includes the civets, genets and mongooses. It is interesting to note that all eight species of carnivore on the island belong to this family, and it is often speculated that they have a common ancestor that very likely came from Africa. The *fosa* can weigh as much as 10 kilograms, but can measure about 2 metres in length on account of a tail that is as long as its body. It is an extremely effective hunter that will take whatever bird or small mammal it can find. Unlike other Malagasy carnivores, its claws are retractile.

The Malagasy striped civet (*Fossa fossana*), locally known as *fanaloka*, is a small, spotted carnivore about the size of a cat. This shy but curious animal is common in the forests of Ankarana and is usually seen at night.

It is not surprising that Ankarana has several species of bat, ranging from the Malagasy fruit bat (*Eidolon helvum dupraneum*) to various small insectivorous species such as *Minopterus inflatus africanus*. Some caves are home to three or four species of bat, and in some the populations are so dense that the entire roof of the cave is a writhing mass of fur. A thin spray of bat faeces and urine rains down

LEFT: *A waterfall cascades over a high cliff in Montagne d'Ambre.*
BELOW: *A chameleon (Furcifer pardalis) in resting position, its prehensile tail curled up.*
OPPOSITE TOP: *Male Furcifer petteri, one of many species of chameleon found in Montagne d'Ambre. The ornamentation on its head is used in territorial displays with other males.*
BOTTOM FAR LEFT: *A Parson's chameleon about to catch an insect. Its moveable eye sockets allow for an accurate aim.*
BOTTOM LEFT: *A giant millipede displays its several hundred pairs of legs, which are operated in wave-form synchrony.*

on the visitor, forming mounds on the cave floor, which support a range of small insects and their predators, such as large poisonous millipedes.

The local Antakarana people have a close relationship with the mountain. The caves have provided refuge for them on various occasions during the course of history. Soldiers of the Merina king, Radama I, pursued local people into the massif where they lived between 1835 and 1838, and several caves still have pottery remains dating from that time. Today the prince of the Antakarana, known as the *ampanjaka*, lives in the village of Ambatoharanana, which is only a few kilometres from the south-western rock wall. A cave on the western side of the mountain functions as a tomb for the royal family.

Sadly, the last few years have seen a powerful onslaught on the mountain of Ankarana and its plants and animals. Sapphires were recently discovered in some of the massif's creeks and within a matter of months tens of thousands of people descended on the area in search of a living. Reports have reached us that one of the troops of crowned lemur (*Eulemur coronatus*) that we photographed recently for this book has been decimated by hunters. Tragically, these curious creatures have become accustomed to scientists, film makers and the occasional tourist, and are now an easy target for unscrupulous hunters and hungry human beings.

Ankarana is one of the last remaining strongholds of nature in the north of Madagascar. Most of the massif now falls within a national park, but it is increasingly difficult for management to cope with the growing population of migrants in the peripheral areas along the eastern side. While people living around the park are hungry, it seems certain that not even the pinnacle fortress of Ankarana will be able to protect nature's irreplaceable treasures.

CHAPTER 8

Represented by a few dots on a world map, lying only four degrees south of the equator, the islands of the Seychelles are a thousand miles from nowhere. Yet these magical islands have often been likened to Paradise. Called "Forever Eden" by the local people, the Seychelles islands have the reputation of being the most beautiful place on earth.

Clear water sparkle in a channel off Aldabra.

Turret corals.

Diverse marine ecosystems off the Seychelles.

A robber crab steals the egg of a green turtle.

THE *Seychelles*

NATURE'S LIVING LABORATORIES

LEFT: *The transparent waters of Cousin Island.* **RIGHT:** *The dark morph of the dimorphic egret (Egretta dimorpha).*

In a remote part of the Western Indian Ocean, between Madagascar and the equator, the islands of the Seychelles lie scattered across the ocean like a string of pearls. These tropical islands are among the most fascinating places in the world, some comprising flat, semi-circular coral atolls, while the ancient granite outcrops of others rise dramatically out of the sea.

The main group of islands, numbering 115 in total, lies about 1 000 kilometres north west of the giant island of Madagascar, and about twice that distance from mainland Africa, making them some of the most isolated in the world. Most of them are so small that one can walk around them in just a few hours. Even Mahé, the largest of the granite islands, is only about 27 km long and about 4 kilometres at its widest point. In all, the total land area of the Seychelles islands is a mere 443 km², spread over about 400 000 km² of Indian Ocean. The number of different islands, coupled with the fact that they have been isolated from the rest of the world for so long, has resulted in an astounding diversity of flora and fauna.

Geological and ecological history

Within the Seychelles archipelago, the unique nature of each island depends to a large extent on how it was formed in distant geological times. The islands of the main group for instance, are granitic outcrops of

ABOVE LEFT: *A mangrove crab feasts on a fallen mangrove leaf.*
ABOVE RIGHT: *A canopy of palm leaves shields out the sun in the Vallée de Mai rainforest.*
FAR LEFT: *The Seychelles tree frog* (Tachynemis seychellensis).
LEFT: *At low tide, the gnarled roots and branches of the mangrove forest on Curieuse Island are exposed.*
OPPOSITE: *Granite outcrops on Curieuse Island.*

a large submarine plateau, some 26 000 square kilometres in extent. These islands tend to rise sharply above the ocean, and the highest one, Mahé, reaches an elevation just short of 1 000 metres. The dramatic appearance of the granitic islands is equalled only by the astonishing richness of floral and faunal species that thrive on them. Wherever one goes, the dense tropical vegetation is alive with the chattering of numerous bird species found nowhere else in the world.

Scientists have long been puzzled as to how these tiny, desolate islands became inhabited with such a rich diversity of species, separated as they are by long distances from other areas with similar habitats. One theory holds that the islands are the crests of a long mountain chain that once connected India and Africa, before the two continents started to drift apart. The ancestors of the species that occur on the islands today are thus thought to originate from the large and varied fauna and flora of the giant land masses of Africa and Asia. Isolated on the Seychelles islands, this rich template of ancestral species slowly evolved into unique forms. Some of these species continued to evolve on the giant island of Madagascar, where, subjected to a different set of forces, they diverged still further. In fact, some birds have become so specialised through time that it is now impossible to trace their ancestry with any degree of accuracy. According to some geologists, much larger areas of the Seychelles islands were once exposed and this may also help to account for the diversity of species found on the shrunken island habitats that remain today.

The origin of the ancient granite rock is also somewhat of a mystery, because the Seychelles is the only group of oceanic islands in the world that are granitic in origin. The rock is pre-Cambrian, some 650 million years old – the same age

as rock found in Madagascar and southern Africa. This similarity further supports the theory that connects the Seychelles islands with Africa and Asia in an age prior to continental drift.

There are reasons other than time and isolation that account for the species richness of the granitic islands. The varied and pronounced topography of the islands gave rise to many different types of habitats, and this wide range of vacant niches promoted the evolution of species to fill them. The habitat diversity of the islands is strongly linked to elevation. At sea level, for example, the beautiful sandy beaches are populated by a variety of creatures that have adapted to life in this soft substrate. Creatures such as burrowing ghost crabs (members of the genus *Ocypode*) dig holes in the sand and remain there all day, appearing on the surface at night to scavenge for debris washed up during the previous high tide. The name of these curious creatures is probably derived from their pale colour and erratic movements, which cause them at times to disappear momentarily from sight as they stop suddenly and wait motionless for danger to pass.

The hermit crab (for example *Coenobita rugosus*) is another remarkable inhabitant of the sandy beaches. These soft-bodied animals live in shells discarded by other crabs, or in old snail shells. As they grow, the hermit crabs periodically have to leave their "borrowed" shells in exchange for roomier homes.

Also at the level of the beaches are large stands of mangroves (including *Avicennia marina*, and at least three other species), trees that are specially adapted to withstand constantly changing water levels and the salty environment. They tend to occur where the sea meets fresh water, such as in the numerous estuaries or in sheltered areas, where they can grow protected from the ocean's moods. Some of the mangrove plants have elongated stilt-like roots that are resilient to wave action and enable the plants to survive even the heaviest of storms. Others are firmly anchored by sprawling buttress roots.

At high tide, only the tops of the trees protrude above the water, and the only visible activity in the mangrove forests may be birds nesting or catching a brief respite in the trees. During low tide, however, the tidal flats and the rich variety of life forms they support are exposed. One of the most common of these inhabitants is the red-clawed mangrove crab. This animal lives in underground tunnels and appears at low tide to scavenge on the muddy surface. The crabs use their agile pincers to pick up the tiniest of food particles, as well as to tear apart the leathery mangrove leaves that have dropped down to the mud.

Various species of mangrove trees exist in the Seychelles. Half water, half land, the mangrove ecosystem is one of the most productive on earth, and provides food and shelter for a host of creatures. Amongst other things, it acts as a nursery for young fish until they are ready to move out into the open ocean. These small fish thrive among the mangrove roots, where they are protected from wave action and larger predators. Here they thrive on the nutrient particles in suspension, while in turn sustaining many sea and shore birds such as herons, boobies and frigate birds.

Above the high tide mark, the island forests begin. The forest floor is damp with leaf litter, and an ideal habitat for ground-dwelling birds. On Cousin Island, for example, the magpie robin busily scratches among the leaves for grubs and other insects. This activity soon attracts the normally lazy, fat skinks of the genus *Mabuya* who wait around eagerly for the right moment to grab their share of the exposed insect life. There are fewer than a hundred pairs of magpie robins left, all of them on Frigate and Cousin Islands. Confusingly, the Seychelles magpie robin (*Copsychus sechellarum*) is neither a magpie nor a robin, but a member of the thrush family.

The little island of Cousin is also home to other unusual birds, such as the fairy tern *(Gygis alba)*. Birds of this species make no nest, but instead lay their spherical eggs directly onto a perch, where they balance precariously. On Cousin Island, the eggs are laid high on the branches where they are out of reach of the voracious

skinks and other predators. Both parents take turns to protect the eggs and although the fairy tern is not a large bird, it is highly defensive and will not hesitate to use its sharp beak to ward off intruders. Only a moment's lapse in attention can be disastrous, and large lizards (such as *Mabuya sechellensis*) are sometimes seen feeding on an egg that has been dislodged and fallen to the ground. Once the young birds are hatched, the very large feet of young fairy terns enable them to walk on branches and cling to perches where few other birds can venture.

The hillsides above the narrow coastal plains afford spectacular views in almost every direction. The blue Indian Ocean meets an irregular shoreline of rocky cliffs or sandy beaches, and from the vantage point of the hillsides other islands can be seen in the distance. On parts of the island of Mahé, deep canyons running up the mountainsides from sea level contrast pleasantly with neatly arranged tea plantations.

The hillsides are also populated by some extraordinary species of indigenous plants. The semi-carnivorous pitcher plant, for example, has specialised leaves with elaborate upright tubular extensions resembling pitchers, at the end of each of which is a half-open lid. These strangely shaped leaves are in fact deadly traps for a range of insects, which are attracted to the sticky nectar on the red underside of the lid. One cannot help watching with ghoulish fascination as a variety of insects, or perhaps a delicate bright green gecko of the genus *Phelsuma*, explores the dangerous openings of the hollow tubes. Insects that become too eager in their thirst for nectar or do not pay enough attention to their positioning, may lose their hold on the slippery surface and end up at the bottom of the hollow tube. The length of the tube and the lid on top of the opening prevent

the insect from taking flight again, and the trapped victim is doomed to die after a prolonged and hopeless struggle. Its rotting body is eventually digested and the nutrients thus released are absorbed by the plant.

With a rise in elevation, the hillside forests quickly become wetter. On the island of Mahé, the effect of altitude on the environment is best experienced by taking a hike up the Gongo Rouge, an exercise that takes the better part of a day. Starting out at the bottom of the gorge, the wanderer is sheltered from the direct sun by a thick canopy. Large *Ficus* trees anchor themselves with sturdy buttress roots that meander across the shallow tropical soil, and the humid forest soon closes in, blocking out the outside world. Creepers hang from the branches of the larger trees, and the round granite boulders are covered with moss. The sound of dripping water and the bubbling of small waterfalls create a fairy tale world that mesmerises the visitor to this ancient environment.

LEFT: *The white-tailed tropic bird (*Phaethon lepturus lepturus*) breeding on Cousin Island.*
BOTTOM LEFT: *Straddling a stream flowing down the Gongo Rouge, the palm* Verschaffeltia splendida *supports itself with stilt roots.*
BELOW RIGHT: *Cloud forest in the Gongo Rouge.*

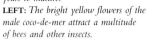

ABOVE: *The green gecko (*Phelsuma sp.*) eats nectar off the rim of the pitcher plant.*
ABOVE LEFT: *The nut of the coco-de-mer is the largest seed in the world, weighing up to 20 kilograms and taking six or seven years to mature.*
LEFT: *The bright yellow flowers of the male coco-de-mer attract a multitude of bees and other insects.*

Vallée de Mai

On the island of Praslin a magnificent palm forest grows along the slopes and in the dark valleys. This is the Vallée de Mai, a true tropical rainforest and home to the extraordinary *coco-de-mer* trees. Not only does the region experience a very high rainfall but palm leaves form a swaying overhead curtain that serves to filter out the dappled sunlight, and keeps the forest moist. The predominant colour of the forest is green, but various shades of yellow and brown mark the older parts of the vegetation. The thick groundcover of decaying material and numerous curtains of vegetation absorb a large amount of the sound generated in the forest, making the forest so quiet that even the gentle whisper of the wind in the trees is audible over the murmur of the numerous creeks that trickle their way down the slopes.

The peace and tranquillity are interrupted occasionally by the whistles of the secretive black parrot (*Coracopsis nigra barklyi*), known locally as *kato nwanr*, which lives largely in the forest canopy. Its call consists of a series of high-pitched whistles that sometimes break up into separate staccato notes and make the bird heard long before it is seen. After its lively call the somewhat drab appearance of this dull brown bird, enlivened only by its orange beak, comes as a surprise. By contrast, other birds of the region are almost regal in appearance. These include the Seychelles blue pigeon (*Alectroenas pulcherrima*), whose prominent red crest and blue-white neck are accentuated by the dark blue feathers of the rest of the bird. Like so many other birds, this pigeon with its deep, coarse, cooing frequents the forest when the stately *Ficus* trees bear fruit.

The Vallée de Mai leaves a lasting impression on all that are fortunate enough to visit this splendid little paradise. When General Charles Gordon first visited the forest in 1881, he was so impressed that he put forward the imaginative theory that this forest must be the site of the original Garden of Eden, and the *coco-de-mer* the Tree of Knowledge. The analogy is perhaps flawed by the presence not of an evil serpent but the Seychelles boa (*Lamprophis geometricus*), a shy creature entirely harmless to humans. In 1983 the Vallée de Mai was declared a World Heritage Site, an apt recognition of the awesome responsibility of mankind to protect environments as unique as these.

The atoll of Aldabra

A green, circular disk in a sea of azure blue, the coral atoll of Aldabra must be one of the loneliest places on earth. Aldabra is located almost 1 000 kilometres south west of Mahé. The island is not granitic in origin, but in fact belongs to a group of islands known as elevated limestone reefs. From the air, it appears first as a tiny speck on the ocean's surface. A closer look shows the atoll (by definition a ring-shaped group of coral islands surrounding a shallow body of water) to consist of four elongated islands encircling a blue-green lagoon. The long slivers of land, known by the exotic-sounding names of Malabar, Polymnie, Picard and Grande Terre, together with the lagoon they encircle, comprise Aldabra. About 34 kilometres in length, it has the distinction of being the largest coral atoll in the world.

The lagoon is drained and filled tidally through narrow channels between the islands. With each receding tide, water flows out into the open sea through channels in the horseshoe-shaped atoll. When the tide is at its lowest, the strange mushroom-like shapes of numerous rocky outcrops stand out in the lagoon, exotic symbols of a normally unseen world.

At low tide, a variety of birds take the opportunity to feast on the mud flats. Many of these, such as the sacred ibis (*Threskiornis aethiopica abbotti*), are suitably equipped with long legs and beaks. Some areas of the lagoon contain large stands of mangroves and thousands of sea birds, such as frigates and boobies, circle overhead. They nest on isolated islands where their offspring can be reared in safety. Like many seabirds, they are able to regulate the salt balance in their systems in spite of a diet heavy in salt through the presence of a special gland that secretes salt.

Like the birds, the mangroves themselves are engaged in a continuous process of desalination. Some species regulate their own salinity by concentrating salt in certain leaves that turn yellow and drop off, thus secreting salt from the tree. The seeds of the mangroves usually drop into the substrate below to germinate, while others are transported by the current to other favourable localities in the lagoon, or out through the numerous channels into the open sea.

Aldabra is thought to derive its name from the Arabic word *al-khadra*, meaning "the green", a name that probably refers to the green reflections of the lagoon on overcast days. Another possibility is that the name comes from another Arabic word, *al-dabaran*, which refers to the five stars in the Taurus group, and may relate to the method of navigation that led to the discovery of the island.

Origins and cycles of life on Aldabra

The ring of coral islands that comprise the atoll of Aldabra are thought to have once surrounded an island which subsequently sank, leaving a shallow lagoon in its place. The living coral that surrounded the island kept growing and today forms the ring of limestone islands surrounding the lagoon. These islands are now the only structures that remain above water, and today the highest rock on the islands, found on Esprit Island, reaches only about 8 metres above sea level. On the island of Grande Terre, storm-blown sand dunes along the shore rise higher.

Surrounding the ancient limestone reef comprising the ring of islands are a profusion of living coral reefs. These reefs are by far the most colourful and diverse ecosystem that occurs in the aquatic environment. The corals themselves are fascinating colonies of tiny animals. At night they feed on nutrient particles, which they filter out with tiny brush-like structures. By day symbiotic algae within the corals convert sunlight into sugars and carbohydrates, by photosynthesis, in exchange for nutrients.

It is this dependence on sunlight that prevents the corals from growing in deep water and restricts them to the shallow coastal waters along tropical shores and islands. The corals secrete calcium carbonate, a hard, rock-like substance that makes up the reef, and members of different species secrete different shapes, thus adding to the structural diversity of the reef. These tiny colonial organisms created the islands making up the atoll and their growth counteracts the forces of erosion, thus maintaining the island above the level of the sea.

Because the island is so flat and low, it has been entirely submerged during various periods of global warming. The last time this occurred was some 125 000 years ago. After each re-emergence of the atoll, terrestrial life had to make a new start on the bare limestone rock, reliant on the currents and winds that brought new species to colonise the lifeless rock.

OPPOSITE LEFT: *Tidal erosion in the lagoon of Aldabra creates strange shapes and tunnels in the limestone.*

OPPOSITE RIGHT: *The mangrove* Bruguieria gymnorhyza *has elongated seeds that drop off and stick in the mud below, where they grow.*

ABOVE: *Aldabra – limestone islands stand out in the lagoon.*

FAR LEFT: *Mushroom-shaped islands appear in the lagoon at low tide, their shapes clearly the result of the weathering of many ages.*

LEFT AND BELOW: *Fossil corals embedded in the limestone hint at the origin of Aldabra. Some date back as far as 118 000 years ago.*

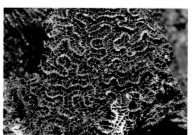

Of course there is no real end to the succession of life on the atoll. The building up of the ecosystem is both continuous and cyclical, with the start of each cycle being marked by the complete submergence of the atoll and its subsequent re-emergence. The time frame in which the cycles occur is difficult to imagine, but the succession of events is probably as follows. Immediately after re-emergence, there would be nothing but bare rock that baked in the sun while the sea constantly eroded away at its outer edges. The next important step would be the gradual formation of soil through weathering and erosion of the rocks, a process that takes place over many thousands of years.

The island would probably first be visited by birds that are able to travel long distances with relative ease, perhaps using the exposed rock as a rest stop on a journey elsewhere. These visitors might carry partially digested seeds in their gut, some of which would still be viable. Some of these capsules, deposited on the primitive soil in a pile of nutrient-rich bird guano, would be the new beginnings of life on the island.

Some of the other early colonisers would probably be marine creatures whose larvae are carried in the ocean currents. Living on the border between sea and land, many of these would be semi-terrestrial forms such as the land crab, today still the most common crab on the island. Where the soil is deep enough, the land crab (*Cardisoma carniflex*) digs moist burrows that provide protection against predators. It also defends itself with its large claws which it opens up at the slightest provocation and carries in front of it like large forklifts. The land crab eats fallen leaves and fruit as well as some young plants, and plays an important role in breaking down vegetable matter and mixing it with the soil, thus adding to the

formation of richer soils. Although entirely capable of holding its own on land, the crab is still dependent on the sea for the development of its eggs, which are carried in a large brown mass under the female's abdomen. At spring tide, female land crabs congregate on the beach to release their eggs into the surf.

After its initial formation, the soil would become progressively richer over time. Eventually it would be able to sustain a large variety of plants, including higher forms such as flowering plants. Today the thick layer of soil present on the island enables three species of ant lion to exist there. One of them is endemic to Aldabra, while the other two occur on mainland Africa as well. The ant lion is a voracious creature with powerful jaws. It lies at the bottom of conical traps of loose sand, waiting for the inevitable hapless ant to fall into the pit. Surprisingly enough, the ant lion is the larvae of lacewings – rather weak creatures resembling damselflies that belong to the order Neuroptera. Other creatures such as mining bees and sand wasps also excavate burrows in the soil.

Smaller creatures, many of which were probably brought to the atoll aloft the trade winds, occupy every part of the terrestrial habitat. At present the atoll contains about 125 different species of Hymenoptera (wasps, bees and ants). The tiny fig wasps (members of the super-family Chalcidoidea), for example, live in symbiotic association with fig trees. The wasps enter the fruit through a tiny opening and lay their eggs in the "flowers" on the inside of the fig, where the larvae are able to hatch and develop in safety from predators. It is not only the wasps that benefit from this behaviour, however. As they move in and out of the fruits, the wasps pollinate the flowers, making this a mutually beneficial relationship for both the wasp and the fig tree.

The turtles of Aldabra

The influence of the sea on Aldabra is never far away. At night, strange creatures are carried from afar to the shore to enact a vital part of their reproductive cycle. Three species of sea turtle occur regularly at Aldabra, namely the green turtle or *orti-d-mer* (*Chelonia mydas*), the hawksbill turtle or *kare* (*Eretmochelys imbricata*), and the logger-head turtle (*Caretta caretta*). Adult green turtles are abundant in the shallow waters along the outer perimeter of the atoll, where they feed, mostly on seagrasses and algae. The hawksbill turtle lives in the coral reefs where it feeds primarily on sponges and algae. Small numbers of loggerhead turtles are found inside the lagoon, and these carnivorous turtles appear to prefer a diet of crustaceans and molluscs.

Both green and hawksbill turtles nest on Aldabra. On virtually every night of the year the green turtle can be seen crawling out onto any one of the 40 sandy beaches recorded thus far as breeding sites. These large creatures may have travelled hundreds – perhaps thousands – of kilometres to deposit their eggs here.

Their nesting activity peaks between May and September, and between 1981 and 1985 there were an estimated 10 000 to 18 000 landings on Aldabra.

The average female green turtle lays three clutches of eggs per season, each one numbering about 150 eggs. Digging a hole with her flippers, laying eggs and then covering them with sand is hard work, and the process can take several hours and sometimes most of the night. Only when her eggs are safely buried under the sand does the female make her way back to the sea.

The hawksbill turtle lays its eggs in broad daylight, never on the same beaches as green turtles, probably to avoid the accidental excavation of their nests by the latter larger species. In the Seychelles the meat of the hawksbill turtle is sometimes poisonous, probably due to the sponges in its diet, and is thus largely avoided. They are nevertheless mercilessly hunted for the exquisite scales that cover their shells, which are prized for jewellery, picture and glasses frames, and combs. Thousands of kilograms of scales have been exported to Japan and this shameful trade still continues today.

Giants of Aldabra

On land, the most remarkable creature that occurs on Aldabra is the giant land tortoise. The presence of these ancient creatures totally dominates the island, where they either rest in the shade or, lumbering slowly across the ground, have the air of being en route to some destination known only to themselves, a determined expression on their prehistoric faces.

TOP: *Having covered her nest with sand, a female green turtle returns to the sea before sunrise.*
ABOVE: *This nest of baby green turtle was uncovered by extreme tides and then preyed upon by birds.*
RIGHT: *A green turtle excavates her egg chamber in the sand. She will lay about 150 eggs in the urn-shaped nesting hole.*

An individual land tortoise weighs up to 400 kilograms and can live to well over 100 years. Its enormous size is a striking example of island giantism. This theory holds that some animals evolve into giant forms on islands, owing to the lack of predators and other constraints that would normally curb their size on the mainland. The opposite phenomenon to giantism is dwarfism, which occurs when certain constraints such as food scarcity or other environmental characteristics promote the evolution of smaller forms than on the mainland. An interesting example of this is the pigmy hippopotamus of Madagascar.

The Aldabra population of the giant land tortoise is the largest in the world, numbering some 150 000 individuals. In fact, they occur in such high densities that Aldabra has a higher biomass than the plains of East Africa with its abundance of large mammals. At present only two species – and several subspecies – of giant tortoise exist worldwide, one in the Galapagos Islands in the Pacific Ocean and the other on Aldabra. Recent studies have dated giant fossil remains on Aldabra at well over 125 000 years old. At a time when people were unable to cross oceans, these fascinating creatures were already traversing the seas.

The dispersal of giant land tortoises to Aldabra was probably purely accidental, and in fact the island was colonised by the tortoises on at least three occasions in the past, each time after re-emergence of the atoll. Tortoises are known to be capable of being dispersed by sea, owing to their waterproof exoskeletons. When they occasionally fall into the sea, perhaps by venturing too near the edge of a crumbling precipice of fossilised coral, their slow metabolic rate and ability to survive long periods without food or water enable them to drift at the mercy of the currents for many weeks, perhaps even months, before finally either perishing or finding land again, where conditions may be favourable for their survival. Females can store sperm for many months, ensuring the perpetuation of the species.

On Aldabra, mating of the tortoises normally occurs between January and May, almost always in the daytime, while egg-laying takes place between June and September, usually at night. The mating sequence is rather unceremonious. Typically a male starts to follow a female. He either catches up with her or is lost in her wake. After catching up with her, he nudges or bites her gently before attempting to mount her. Once on top of the female, he moves around until his concave belly plates fit over her curved carapace. The male then rises on his back legs and moves back and forth, while his tail searches for her cloaca. If found, the male inserts his penis into the cloaca and completes transfer of sperm. During the mounting stage the male regularly emits a series of characteristic groans that can be heard over a distance of hundreds of metres.

Fertilised eggs are usually laid at night. The female digs a hole with her hind legs, and urinates in it. The urine contains a mucus that lines the hole, hardening as it dries into a protective layer. The eggs themselves are about the size of an

FAR LEFT: A giant land tortoise feeds on dry leaves. These animals must sometimes withstand long periods of drought.
LEFT: Tortoises grazing on the atoll of Aldabra maintain the green "lawns" known as tortoise turf.
BELOW: Giant land tortoises mating on Aldabra. Their mating calls can be heard over hundreds of metres.

ABOVE LEFT: *A land crab deposits her eggs in the surf during spring tide.*
ABOVE CENTRE: *The Aldabra fruit bat (Pteropus seychellensis aldabrensis) rests in the shade of a tree.*
ABOVE RIGHT: *The great frigate bird (Fregata minor) breeds in colonies of up to 30 000 birds on Aldabra.*
RIGHT: *The black and white beetle (Mausoleopsis aldabrensis) is an important pollinator of many plants.*
OPPOSITE: *The white form of the dimorphic egret (Egretta dimorpha) patrols the shore-line for small fish and washed-up food.*

orange, and up to 16 are laid in a clutch. Once laid, they too are urinated upon, and then incubated in the warm sand. Between 73 and 160 days later, depending on the time of the year, the eggs hatch into soft-shelled hatchlings – easy prey for crabs and rats.

Giant land tortoises control their temperature by basking in the shade during the day. In the afternoon, they often face east, so that they can feed in their own shade. At night they sleep with their necks extended and in the open, as there are no predators to fear.

The giant tortoises are the largest herbivores on the island, and distinguish Aldabra from any other environment on earth, since here the largest animal is a reptilian herbivore whereas elsewhere that place is reserved for mammals. On Aldabra, the tortoises have an enormous impact on the appearance of their environment: they maintain extensive patches of short grass resembling lawns, known as "tortoise turf". They also maintain a browse line reminiscent of that on the African plains, where it is maintained by the taller ruminants such as giraffe. Tortoise dung is the start of a food chain that incorporates flies, hermit crabs and other scavengers. In this sense the hermit crabs fulfil the role of the dung beetle on the African continent. The tortoises also support a healthy population of mosquitoes that descend on the unprotected areas of their bodies, depending on the tortoise's blood for survival and reproduction.

Another impressive giant of the island is the coconut crab, *Birgus latro*, a giant hermit crab without a shell. The adults attain enormous sizes, with adult males measuring up to a metre across from leg tip to leg tip, and as such are possibly the largest terrestrial arthropods in the world. Their sturdy, machine-like build and extraordinary size give them an air of science fiction. They show little fear and can drag around a coconut weighing several kilograms. They feed on a variety of plant material and living, dead or decaying animal material such as eggs and dead animals that are washed ashore. In spite of their size, the crabs are able to ascend coconut trees, their spiky claws finding an easy grip on the bark. Their pincers are powerful enough to sever the leathery stipe of a coconut, and they are able to tear off the husk in no time.

For many species, life on Aldabra is a constant struggle for survival. The climate is hot and humid, as Aldabra lies not far south of the equator. Rainfall is not high, however, because the island is located in a relatively low rainfall area in the Indian Ocean, and in spite of the green of the vegetation, water is scarce here.

Other creatures of the atoll

Due to Aldabra's isolation and the rigours of the environment, there are no indigenous mammals on the island other than bats, which are able to fly there. Four bat species have been identified on the island. Only one of them is endemic, a fruit bat (*Pteropus aldabrensis*), while the other three insectivorous bats are not. Very little is known about the other three species of bats and they have not been on Aldabra long enough to evolve into new subspecies.

Like many of the land bird species on the islands, the fruit bats show little fear, as they evolved in isolation from diurnal predators. During the day they roost, hanging upside down, and because large numbers of bats roost together in close proximity, and because unwilling females hanging upside down on a branch are unable to escape quickly, rape is a fairly common event. The wings of the fruit bat comprise large flaps of skin strung between enormously enlarged "finger" bones, which form an expandable frame. At night they fly off to look for ripening fruits, and there are records of fruit bats eating the fruit of all three *Ficus* species on the island, as well as that of *Mystroxylon aethiopicum*, a common shrub that bears red fruits throughout the year. The fruit bat is to some extent in competition with birds such as the Comoro blue pigeon (*Alectroenas sganzini minor*), although this competition is reduced because the birds feed in the day time while the bats are nocturnal.

Far below the roosts of the bats, however, it is the flightless Aldabra or white-throated rail (*Dryolimnas cuvieri aldabranus*) that epitomises the isolation of the atoll. Today it lives only on Polymnie and Malabar, where it feeds on crustaceans, small lizards, tortoise eggs and insects. This handsome bird is the last surviving flightless bird of the Indian Ocean, a region once famous for its flightless forms. Today, the dodo of Mauritius is extinct, as is the solitaire of Réunion and the elephant bird of Madagascar. The Aldabra flightless rail survived only because of the extreme remoteness of the Aldabra atoll. Having taken an evolutionary course that led to the loss of its flying ability, the rail's destiny is now locked into the islands of Polymnie and Malabar. No longer able to disperse even across short distances of water, let alone to other islands in the Indian Ocean, the Aldabra rail is destined to live out the rest of its existence on these tiny specks of land in the Indian Ocean.

Paradise in the Western Indian Ocean

One of the richest and most alluring corners of the western Indian Ocean lies between the African mainland and the island states of the Seychelles and Madagascar. Unlike Africa's Atlantic coast, which is frequently battered by storms and enormous surges, the Western Indian Ocean experiences relatively calm conditions throughout much of the year. The clear, warm tropical waters, the white sandy beaches and the beautiful coral reefs along this coast epitomise paradise in the tropics and draw travellers from all over the world.

Diving in a coral reef must one of the most exhilarating experiences a human being can have. There is within the reef a dazzling array of colours and forms, and an assemblage of creatures so diverse that the coral reef is sometimes referred to as the rainforest of the sea. Indeed, coral reefs have more species per unit area than any other marine system. Interestingly, while they do not have as many species as rainforests, they have a larger representation of phyla.

Corals are coelenterates, which means they belong to the same group of animals as sea anemones and jellyfishes. The corals are tiny colonial polyps, and when they reproduce the new individual remains attached to the parent. With the continual formation of more polyps, a cluster is formed. The reef-building corals, known as the Sclerectinia, secrete the characteristic shapes of hard calcium carbonate that make up the reef. New polyps grow over old ones, stifling them and adding on new layers of calcium carbonate secretions, thereby contributing to the girth of the colony.

Corals feed at night by means of stinging nematocysts, withdrawing into their hard exoskeletons by day. Each polyp catches and digests its own food particles, but the nutrition passes to the entire colony. Corals also incorporate into their own bodies tiny single-cell plants known as zoocanthellae, which convert sunlight to energy through photosynthesis and also consume carbon dioxide produced by the coral. Thus most coral species grow best near the surface and never in water deeper than 75 metres.

The reef also provides shelter for countless other creatures, including hundreds of species of fish, eels, octopus, and a multitude of invertebrates. Most coral reefs, representing approximately 6 000 years of growth during the most recent period of sea-level rise, have an average vertical growth of about 3 millimetres per year. They are the oldest and largest biogenic structures in nature, their ancient skeletons holding detailed archaeological records over a vast span of time.

Today one can sail along the Mozambique and Tanzania coasts for long distances and still feel like the first visitor to this majestic coastline. Yet the end of this paradise might well be imminent. Unsustainable patterns of fishing, dynamiting of the coral reefs, slash and burn agriculture, increased sedimentation from deforestation and poorly managed tourism are taking their tragic toll on the coastal habitat. On the bright side, however, both countries now have a new generation of talented and motivated planners who are involved in promising programmes with international donors, in particular the Swedish government. A further encouraging sign is that East African countries and island states are now working together on guidelines for integrated coastal development, including mariculture operations and tourism.

ABOVE: *A longnose hawkfish* (Oxycirrhites typus) *hovers near a gorgonian seafan.*
RIGHT: *The anemonefish* (Amphiprion chrysogaster) *has a symbiotic relationship with the sea anemone which it cleans in return for protection.*

FAR LEFT: *The big longnose butterflyfish* (Forcipiger longirostris).
CENTRE: *Turret coral (Dendrophyllia sp.) is a soft coral that does not secret calcium carbonate.*
LEFT: *The frogfish* (Antennarius sp.).
OVERLEAF: *The blue-faced angel fish* (Pomacanthus xantometopon).

A CONTINENT IN TRANSITION

The Edens that formed the basis of this book are but a handful of the many areas of incredible beauty and biodiversity that still exist in the African continent and its associated islands. Their exploration led to a range of spectacular places and to our observation of many different aspects of these unique places. From the Cape Peninsula in South Africa to the remote coral atoll of Aldabra in the Seychelles and the moist tropical forests of Uganda, the overwhelming and ever-present realisation was always that Africa is a continent in a state of transition.

Enormous changes are sweeping across the continent, including, in many countries, fundamental polit-ical and economic changes. These are often of such magnitude that they appear to override many of the other maladies associated by the western world with the continent, such as poverty, disease and war. It is thus inevitable that the Last Edens of this book, even the most remote, have already been or will in the future be affected by these changes. Thus, along with an appreciation of their beauty, their diversity, their innate "Africanness", lurks the knowledge that these Edens are all under threat, and their survival into the near future seems ever less secure. In the light of this, it seems appropriate to examine some of them more closely, and attempt to assess their chances of survival under conditions of still higher pressures, including the threat of populations set to double over the next 50 years.

That all of the Last Edens are under threat became chillingly clear during the compilation of this book. The Bwindi Impenetrable Forest, for example, home to over half of the remaining world population of mountain gorillas, rises as a small forest island out of a sea of plantations and settlements. Its preservation is conditional upon its ability to offer real financial spin-offs to those who would otherwise carve it up for farmland. Although the gorillas do indeed offer such incentives, it is a sobering thought that a reserve almost wholly reliant on but a single species for its survival, rests on inherently shaky ground.

A similar situation exists in northern Madagascar, in the ancient limestone fortress of hidden forests linked by networks of caves, that comprises Ankarana. This region, recently declared a national park, is a stronghold for many species of plants and animals, some of which are found nowhere else in the world. In spite of its theoretically conserved status, however, at the time of writing this book the area was under siege from tens of thousands of settlers, intent on mining for sapphires. Desperate to escape the growing poverty that threatens a country already beset with environmental problems, that range from topsoil erosion to overgrazing, the people leap for an opportunity to provide themselves with even short-term financial relief. As in Bwindi, the survival of the park into the future is highly dependent on the co-operation of the local inhabitants, for whom conservation often entails heavy personal costs, such as loss of land or access to resources, for example, which they can ill afford. In addition to attempting to meet the requirements of local people, conservation areas such as these are also dependent on national priorities, which, in developing world countries, do not always include conservation of biodiversity at the top of the list.

The situation in Namaqualand is somewhat different. This region is blessed with a dramatic coastline that has remained largely pristine by virtue of the security fences erected to restrict access to the diamond mines of the region by outsiders. While the diamond mining itself has caused considerable damage to the land surfaces, particularly in those parts with particularly rich diamond deposits, it has also provided temporary protection from other types of development. Today, there exists a chance to put in place a system of effective coastal management in which development and conservation can be balanced. Inland, the region comprises riverine canyons, a mountain desert of astonishing biodiversity and vast desert plains with unique plants and animals. In addition, it is also an area rich in cultural diversity.

Socially and economically, one of the most significant problems faced by Namaqualand at present is the imminent depletion of the land-based diamond deposits. Since the mines are the largest source of employment in the area, this is likely to have a tremendous impact on the region. In the absence of other viable alternatives, large numbers of workers will almost certainly turn to the land to make a living – a recipe for disaster in a semi-arid region where the carrying capacity for livestock is inherently low, and where rainfall is too low to allow for much successful cultivation of the land. Other former mine labourers will be forced to join the ever-growing stream of people leaving the rural areas for the cities, in search of a better livelihood. Either way, the environmental and social costs will be heavy.

On a more positive side, however, efforts are being made by several organisations, including mining houses, government and non-government agencies and the South African National Parks, to move the area away from an economy based on the non-renewable and diminished diamond resource to a nature-based economy. If this succeeds, the new economic driving forces of the region are likely to be tourism and the harvesting and cultivation of marine resources. The coastline here is rich in algal and other intertidal organisms, including mussels and limpets, that are commercially harvested elsewhere in the world. The potential for mariculture is also great and at least one mine has made preliminary attempts to cultivate oysters in old mining blocks. In addition to these valuable resources, the region, being one of the few desert biodiversity "hot spots" in the world, also has the potential to support a strong form of nature-based tourism.

Thus in terms of both conservation and socio-economics, the future of Namaqualand is potentially bright. Mining activity has resulted in a reasonable infrastructure already being in place, and the region is but sparsely populated. If managed properly and according to a well-conceived environmental economic plan, the region ought to be able to feed and sustain the other needs of the local inhabitants into the future. Local communities are becoming increasingly aware of the need to develop sustainable livelihood options and by and large support attempts to create a lattice of coastal and inland parks that will attract discerning, paying ecotourists from around the world. However, a real danger is that, once

again, both the control of and benefits accruing from the utilisation of coastal resources and tourism will fall into the hands of outsiders. As in all the cases discussed so far, it is only if the local inhabitants of Namaqualand are given a significant stake in such developments that the future of one of the most beautiful of the Last Edens can be assured.

One of the most compelling of the Last Edens is the Okavango Delta in Botswana. This wetland is unequalled when it comes to a habitat supporting the continent's large mammals. When the waters reach the delta at the start of winter, thousands of migratory antelope descend upon the delta in search of water and grazing, attracting in turn an array of large predators. Over the last few years, however, the delta has been radically altered, its wetlands cleared to create grazing for cattle, its waters tapped to supply burgeoning towns and industries, its very heart penetrated by safari camps and game lodges.

The attraction of the delta in terms of tourism is hardly surprising. Africa's large mammals, so abundant in the Okavango, fuel the desire of those inhabitants of the industrialised nations who can afford to travel the long distance to Africa, to see them at least once. Today, the area is under immense pressure from over 90 tourism companies operating there. Most of these companies are owned by outsiders, a fact that necessarily curbs the benefits derived by local people from the tourism, while the physical toll exerted by tourism on the fragile land is clearly visible, in spite of gallant efforts by the Botswana Wildlife Service to manage and control the new wave of invaders. In the classic tragedy of tourism, there is a real danger that the Okavango Delta will be consumed by its own beauty.

More ominous threats hang over the serene wetlands of the Okavango Delta. The Okavango River and delta system impinge on three different countries. Starting in the highlands of Angola, the river flows through the Caprivi, a panhandle protruding eastwards from Namibia, before entering Botswana, from where it fans out across the northern Kalahari Desert to form its delta. The thirsty neighbouring country of Namibia, which does not benefit from the presence of the beautiful swamps of Botswana, has laid out plans to siphon off large quantities of water from the Okavango River for its own needs. This highlights the imperative need for the Okavango system to be seen as a holistic entity, a fragile and finely balanced system that belongs not necessarily to one country, but is viewed as an irreplaceable global asset. At the very least, a form of integrated management should be implemented, with the agreement of all major role players and which carries the support of the local inhabitants of the entire region. Even then, the future of the Okavango Delta is far from secure, and the risk that it will slip away into yet another "once were Edens" is a real one.

Other than burgeoning population growth, one of the most obvious dangers to the Last Edens and the areas surrounding them is the importation of inappropriate technology, which may appear at first as the solution to a particular problem but in reality may bring with it devastating environmental effects. A particularly good example of this is the introduction of the nylon fishing net to the Masoala Peninsula in Madagascar. Traditionally, women and children fished with woven traps. Today, however, nylon nets dominate fishing practices, and almost everyone who can afford a net has one. The nets are dragged across the floor of the shallow lagoons with great effect, their mesh size so small that large numbers of most fish species present in the waters are caught long before they are large enough to breed. Furthermore, the dragging action of the nets inflicts serious damage on the coral beds themselves, destroying the very habitat that sustains the valuable marine resources.

More than just inappropriate technology threatens the future of the Masoala Peninsula, however. The population is growing rapidly, both because of a high birth rate and because of the rate of influx of migrants, moving there in search of a better future. Already the forest is disappearing at a rate of about 6 per cent per year, and, surprisingly, in view of the fact that Madagascar has already lost over 90 per cent of its indigenous forests, a logging company has recently been awarded a contract to clear-cut a remaining large section of forest in Masaola. Thus a real danger exists that in a few decades the last remnants of forest may occur only along the steepest slopes and in the deepest valleys. One positive step against this is, however, the delineation of a sizeable section of Masoala as a national park, along with the three marine reserves already in existence. Unfortunately, the latter exist only on paper, in the absence of any capacity for reserve management amongst the local people. A sad aspect of many of the aid organisations that have been active in the region for a number of years is their apparent concern with their own survival, rather than with environmental education of the local people or the building of management capacity among the local people to take effective control over their own dwindling resources.

As has already been suggested, one of the greatest dangers to the Last Edens is, ironically, tourism itself. International nature-based tourism is essentially a process whereby visitors from the industrialised nations pay a portion of their expendable cash to the developing world for a chance to see the biodiversity that still exists there. While tourism can play an important financial role in sustaining such places, the fact that the industry is largely in the hands of commercial businesses means that profit making usually assumes a higher priority than environmental or sociological concerns. Consequently inappropriate tourism development is a common sight, particularly along the magical tropical beaches that line the East African coast. Unfortunately, tourism development guidelines and the means to enforce them are largely lacking in the developing world, although efforts are underway to examine ways of steering tourism development in a sustainable direction. The extent to which these measures can actually be applied in real life remains to be seen, but it is at least a start. Individuals can play their part in putting in place sustainable tourism by choosing tour operators with clear environmental guidelines and who show a commitment to the local communities in the areas in which they operate.

Not all the changes that are sweeping the continent are bad, however. For many decades Africa has been associated in the eyes of the western world with brutal wars, pervasive poverty and debilitating diseases. This view is slowly changing in the face of unprecedented positive developments on the continent. Africa today has more leaders of state that were democratically elected than ever before. For the first time in history its economic growth of 4 per cent is higher than its population growth. South Africa, previously the apartheid pariah of this world, is presently undergoing a metamorphosis from a country locked into the oppressive policies of the past into one that has the potential to extend a positive influence to the frontline states around it and far beyond.

Today there is a growing realisation inside and outside the continent that Africa is coming of age in the global environment and should be assisted in assuming the important role it will play in the future of the planet. Whereas previously astronomical sums of aid money were made available by the industrialised nations for ill-conceived projects, there at least now exist better guidelines on how to channel such money more effectively, although such projects are by no means a thing of the past. More funding agencies are becoming aware that money is not the easy solution to every problem it was once thought to be. There is a growing realisation that projects must be carefully chosen and designed with the input of local people.

With the realisation of the importance of involving the local communities, considerable efforts are being made by many industrialised nations and world agencies such as the Global Environment Fund (GEF) to apply funding to projects that will show positive results. The more successful ones, such as some of those along the East African coast, supported by the Swedish government, espouse a strong ethic of pervasive community involvement. At the heart of such projects lies the building of the capacity of the local people themselves, so that they can make informed decisions that will enable them to manage their environmental problems effectively. Solutions imported from America and Europe seldom work in Africa. This does not mean that technical help should not be accepted with the same enthusiasm that it is usually intended. However, it is of paramount importance that the people of Africa develop both the expertise and confidence to find and apply innovative solutions to the continent's problems. Only then will Africa have the ability to determine its own trajectory to a sustainable future.

LEFT: *Black clouds promise rain to the dusty Moremi landscape in the Okavango Delta.*

REFERENCES

Amin, M., Willetts, D. and Skerrett, A. 1995. *Aldabra. World Heritage Site.* Nairobi: Camerapix Publishers.

Branch, G.M. and Branch, M. 1995. *The living shores of southern Africa.* Cape Town: Struik Publishers.

Cowling, R. (ed.). 1992. *The ecology of fynbos. Nutrients, fire and diversity.* Cape Town: Oxford University Press.

Estes, R. 1992. *The safari companion.* Halfway House: Russell Friedman.

Fossey, D. 1983. *Gorillas in the mist.* London: Hodder and Stoughton.

Fraser, M. 1994. *Between two shores. Flora and fauna of the Cape of Good Hope.* Cape Town: David Philip.

La Croix, I.F. 1983. *Malawi orchids: Volume 1. Epiphytic orchids.* Rotterdam: Balkema.

Langrand, O. 1990. *A guide to the birds of Madagascar.* New Haven: Yale University Press.

Le Roux, A. and Schelpe, E.A.C.L.E. 1981. *Namaqualand and Clanwilliam. South African Wild Flower Guide.* Cape Town: Botanical Society of South Africa.

Lewis, D., Reinthall, P. and Trendall, J. 1986. *A Guide to the fishes of the Lake Malawi National Park.* Switzerland: World Wildlife Fund.

Lovegrove, B. 1993. *The living deserts of Southern Africa.* Cape Town: Fernwood Press.

Main, M. 1987. *Kalahari. Life's variety in dune and delta.* Halfway House: Southern Book Publishers.

Penny, M. 1992. *The birds of the Seychelles and the outlying islands.* London: Collins.

Preston-Mafham, K. 1991. *Madagascar – a natural history.* Cape Town: Struik Publishers.

Roodt, V. *The Shell field guide to the common trees of the Okavango Delta and Moremi Game Reserve.* Botswana: Shell.

Ross, K. 1987. *Jewel of the Kalahari: Okavango.* London: BBC Books.

Stoddart, D.R. 1984. *Biography and ecology of the Seychelles islands.* Netherlands: Junk Publishers.

Williams, J.G. and Arlott, N. 1980. *A field guide to the birds of East Africa.* London: Collins.

Wilson, J. 1995. *Lemurs of the lost world.* London: Impact Books.

PHOTOGRAPHIC CREDITS

INDEX

*Page numbers in **bold** refer to photographs.*

132